Stories we tell…

Experiences in coaching, work, and life

JIM CONSTABLE

&

KIM HORSTMANSHOF

"Some stories are your responsibility. They come to you because you're the only person who can tell them."

ALICE WALKER

CONTENTS

We have categorised the stories in the hope of helping the reader. Few of you will read this book from front to back, reading every word in order. We hope that the categories enable you to dip into different parts, around a particular topic or context.

There are some stories that fit in more than one category. There are obvious overlaps between, say, attitude, goals and being all you can be. Hopefully the headings below make sense and the stories within them are about right.

"Our bodies are garbage-heaps: we collect experience, and from the decomposition of the thrown-out eggshells, spinach leaves, coffee grinds, and old steak bones of our minds come nitrogen, heat, and very fertile soil.

Out of this fertile soil bloom our poems and stories.

But this does not come all at once.

It takes time.

Continue to turn over and over the organic details of your life until some of them fall through the garbage of discursive thoughts to the solid ground of black soil."

NATALIE GOLDBERG

THANK YOU

I would like to thank all those who have employed me or had me as their coach – tolerating me and hopefully benefitting from our work together. I've learned so much.

Thank you too to my wife Rachel for her support and encouragement, and to Rachel, Barry, Kuen, Nick and others for their ideas, input and reading of drafts.

Jim

Firstly, thanks to those of you who read our draft, especially Erica, and gave us incredibly helpful feedback– your suggestions were invaluable.

Secondly, I want to thank Jim for asking me to work on this book with him and his patience with how long it has taken me to write my parts!

Thirdly, I'd like to thank everyone who has helped me learn and grow, whether my family, friends, teachers, colleagues, or teammates. Without you none of my stories would exist and I wouldn't be half the person I am today. From school to New Zealand, university to work to rugby and beyond; the people who have surrounded me have taught me so much and I am grateful beyond words.

Finally, a special thanks to the yellow rose crew, and particularly the teller of tall tales about Tigers in Twickenham.

Kim

HOW TO USE THE STORIES IN THIS BOOK

Do stories always have a purpose? I suppose bedtime stories are meant to be relaxing and horror stories to cause excitement. Many stories are told in order to stimulate a feeling or emotion.

Some are told so that we don't forget important times or lessons from our past.

Others are told to convey a sense of belonging. Perhaps we hear a story that reminds us of ourselves and that is a comfort to us – that others made the same mistake or experienced the same trials and tribulations.

We also hear stories that change our mind about something or prompt action, whether in a work setting or any other part of our lives. Perhaps we have been mulling something over but a story we hear is the stimulus for us to act.

The stories in this book could do any of the above, including sending you to sleep!

To 'use' the stories in this book – whether in work or life – you will need to relate them to your own experience in some way. In some cases the link might be obvious but in others you might need to pause and think for a moment.

Just about all of the stories in this book are literal – they actually happened. They are not tall tales! But many powerful stories are indeed apocryphal. Where the stories in this book do relate – or you can relate to them enough (like the apocryphal ones) they might make you see a situation through a fresh pair of eyes and cause you to see options that you couldn't see before.

It might be, too, that telling one of these stories to someone else –

family, friend or work colleague - is the most powerful and effective way for you to communicate to them what you are thinking and how you are feeling. A story can be a way of sharing something or communicating a message in a way that you might otherwise be struggling to find the words to do.

These stories are a way of communicating either with yourself, or with others, in the home or in the workplace.

INTRODUCTIONS

JIM

My life has been one of ordinariness. Did well at school - sports, exams – and, typically, didn't know what direction to go in. Went to university, got a job, got married and had a family.

When I was 28 I was invited to apply for a job in a training department; this was life changing. From an introverted, slightly nerdy - ever so slightly mind - young adult, what has become a lifetime of learning, reflection and new experiences has made me the person I am.

I've been a coach, consultant and trainer for over 25 years. One part of the advice, or methodology, I've come to use, is about playing to strengths. To me this means Be You, and one of the stories below is about exactly that. And I've come to realise that I have an ability to remember stuff, and that stuff is such a useful word. And often in conversations, people say things that remind me of that stuff. And in that way I've gathered, rehearsed and told, given and shared, a healthy number of stories, examples and anecdotes.

What I am certain about of stories, from my own direct experience, is a few things. They have been around for a long time - thousands of years. They are told for various reasons - for entertainment, for comfort (because they can be remembered) and as a way of passing on knowledge. They are told to convey meaning - to help people learn, as examples, as comparisons, to give ideas, as ways of offering perspective and of stimulating new thinking.

There are some I've told many times. Most are from my own personal experience - nearly failing my first year at university for example - and some are ones I remember which I retell, as has long been the way with stories.

I've been meaning to write these down for some time. They are grouped them into subjects to give them some kind of order. Several could have been in more than one category. I hope you like them, find them interesting, even meaningful, and maybe choose to retell them.

I'm also led to believe that as we retell stories over the years our memory changes them and a bias emerges which means that, with repetition, we tend to retell them increasingly in our own favour. Forgive me.

I'm delighted that Kim Horstmanshof agreed to collaborate with me. I like Kim's writing, her calm, insightful manner and above all another perspective to add to my own. I simply asked her to read each story and to add anything she had to say. I feel her voice adds something to my own and I'm thankful to her for a sustained effort in making her significant contribution.

You will notice that lots of Kim's pieces end with a question or two. No bad thing. My stories tend to just finish, and hang in the air, perhaps the silence inviting a thought or response. If I were to make a recommendation it would be to pause momentarily after each one – a task in itself that will likely require effort in an ever increasingly busy world – and see what comes to mind.

I hope the stories give you perspective, maybe inspiration and maybe prompt a helpful thought or two. Above all I hope you enjoy the stories whether you read one of them or all 115 of them.

JIM CONSTABLE

KIM

When Jim asked if I'd be interested in collaborating with him on this book, I was honoured but also a bit perplexed. Jim has been working as a coach and trainer for many years, telling stories and understanding what makes people stop, think, and reflect. I wasn't sure my wanderings through the world of work over the last decade or two had quite the same value as material for a book!

My current job is in knowledge management. What's that, you ask? Well, when I had a joiner and his apprentice fitting some doors, they asked me about my work. I asked the joiner if he told his apprentice how he approaches difficult tasks, and whether he talks the apprentice through the decisions that he takes? He said that he did. I asked him if he told the apprentice stories of really tricky jobs where he managed to find a solution, or of the days when everything went really wrong, and how it got fixed? He said that he did. I told him that people in offices don't always do that, and it's my job to help them share their experiences and knowledge. Telling stories – especially when they're about challenging experiences or interesting successes – is a great and time-honoured way of learning from those around us. And it is usually pretty enjoyable too!

I first met Jim in 2015, when he was leading a cohort of staff through an organisational high performance programme that lasted for about a year. I came into the programme quite cynical about a high performance sport-related approach as something that would help me at work, despite having a decade of medium-level amateur rugby under my belt.

By the end of that year I'd learned a lot about myself and my approach to work. I became eager and curious to learn and understand more about what drives us personally and professionally. I started reading a lot of business and high-performance focused articles, sharing what I was reading with the rest of the cohort every week. Over time, that sharing became a weekly email that has very much evolved over the years. These days it rarely includes links to other articles but tends to be a mixture of my own thoughts and reflections, interspersed with amusing pictures/memes – the latter being the primary attraction for many recipients!

Jim has been receiving these emails from the start; providing valuable feedback and very often responding to my thoughts or rhetorical questions with stories, thoughts and experiences of his own. Sometimes my emails are dashed out in haste; the focus is getting them sent before my self-imposed deadline of Friday at 5pm. Jim's questions and thoughts make me reflect on what I've written, consider his perspective, and frequently ask another question. I've come to deeply value this co-reflective practice which gives me new perspective on my thoughts and questions, and allows me to explore them in greater detail.

Jim frequently writes on LinkedIn, and from time to time he'll pick up on a point I've made and explore it in his writing, and vice versa. So when we explored how to add the extra voice he was looking for to his stories, we decided to continue developing this practice we've accidentally honed over the years, and read each other's stories and ask questions. You'll see the questions and thoughts and comments at the end of each story (and once or twice you'll find Jim and I have swapped roles, and he has responded with his thoughts to my story).

KIM HORSTMANSHOF

Storytelling is the most powerful way to put ideas into the world today.

ROBERT MCKEE

1 ATTITUDE

"Life shrinks or expands according to one's courage."

ANAIS NIN

"Until you make the unconscious conscious, it will direct your life and you will call it fate."

JUNG

"Failure is a bruise, not a tattoo."

"Chance favours the prepared mind."

PASTEUR

A sunny disposition is worth more than fortune. Young people should know that it can be cultivated; that the mind like the body can be moved from the shade into the sunshine."

ANDREW CARNEGIE

Behaviour follows attitude and so it feels appropriate to start with some stories about attitude. When it comes to performance, attitude, and mindset, are massive contributing factors. Time spent here is very worthwhile.

The first story is a very personal one, about a challenging time of my life when I was looking proper failure in the face for probably the first time.

Failing my first year and what happened next

I did well at maths at school. It was like problem solving and doing puzzles, though I'm not sure how much I really understood it.

At A-level I had a maths teacher whose students were challenged to sink or swim. Despite (or because of?) his uncompromising style I got an A which played a big part in me getting into Loughborough to do a joint honours degree in PE (Sports Science) and Maths

However the first year of degree maths was hard! I would sit in lectures on some subjects not understanding anything. Nothing. Much of it was gobbledygook. I know I got a bit dispirited.

At the end of the first year, to progress to year two, you had to average 40% in the end of year exams and not get lower than 30% on any single exam. When the results came out I had scored 15% on one paper! 15%!!! And it wasn't in a subject that I thought I would do that badly in. I was horrified. I was shocked and scared that I would get thrown out. My thoughts kept going to my parents and what they would think.

To my (partial) relief I was offered a potential way out. I was asked to attend a viva – an oral interview exam – with the tutor for that particular subject, plus the overall course tutor and a third lecturer, Stan Sherman, who was quirky and likeable and had always been friendly towards me. Mr Sherman had told us on day one that completing a degree was less about the knowledge acquired and more about what it said for our ability to study, learn and persevere. I think he was right.

So the interview felt like a big deal with a lot riding on it. It felt like there was everything to lose and I was a nervous wreck. It was only by convincing myself that they wanted to let me through to the second year anyway that I overcame my nerves enough to turn up and say my name at the start. After all, they could have simply failed me and not given me this second chance.

They told me to take my time, writing down anything I wanted to on a pad of paper before answering their questions. I couldn't answer the first question, having to say, "I'm sorry, I don't know". They said "ok, let's go back to basics and start with a simpler one". I couldn't answer anything as I couldn't think. Finally, at the end, Stan Sherman asked his only question – an easy set up – which I was able to get right. My memory is that it was the only question I answered.

So when they let me through, 'relieved' was not the word. I was so much more than that. I was determined not to go through that trauma again. So at the start of the second year I resolved *to be the perfect student*. I've no idea where that came from. But it worked.

Being *the perfect student* meant several things to me. It meant still enjoying student life: socialising, going to the pub and playing sports. It meant playing a little less cards and watching less rubbish on TV, so less time wasted. And it meant in lectures, asking questions and doing any recommended extra reading, sometimes asking if there was anything else to do. In practice, the attitude led to discipline and application.

A boy called Stephen Thomas joined us in our second year having failed his first year and retaken it. When I was sitting at the front of a lecture, making notes, asking questions and trying to be *the perfect student*, he would look at me thinking I was nuts, and not able to work me out. It was a strategy – the perfect student bit – that was part attitude, part act and part way of motivating myself.

At the end of my second year, which counted 40% of my degree, I got a 2:2 and was delighted. In my final year I worked harder still - to try and keep up with other course mates - and in the end I got a 2:1.

The whole experience taught me so much: the importance of attitude, that I could work hard and maybe that I was lucky too. Whilst they weren't lessons that I applied from then on every day to everything I did (I can be a slow learner) they were things that served me well in the future.

I don't know where choosing an attitude, let alone "be a perfect student" came from. But, with hindsight, it was my first definite and clear example of deliberately choosing my mindset and afterwards on reflection being confident that it made a significant difference to my behaviour.

Jim's story about his classmates reminded me of a particular experience in my own school career. I was in the final year of my very small primary school; I'd always been at the top end of the class in terms of academic ability, but my terrible handwriting, poor maths skills, and tendency to get distracted often played against me. However, with only 14 of us in our year group and mixed age-classes, I don't think I'd stood out particularly.

For some reason, that changed in our final year, as my friend Liz and I started to be called 'swots', 'nerds' and 'geeks' by our classmates. It was a bit upsetting, but our parents were keen for us to work hard and focus on the move to secondary school, knowing that we were the only two of our class who wanted to go to the local girls-only high school. They advised us to ignore the name-calling and tried to encourage us to see these expressions as thinly disguised admiration, or jealousy.

One day around this time, the class took a maths test. Despite me having no great skills in maths, one of my classmates copied my answers and shared them with the other girls. When the results were handed out and it turned out my answer was wrong, they all turned and blamed me for ruining their tests.

I'm not sure I realised at the time that I should only be answerable to myself for my performance and not anyone else. In hindsight, however, it's pretty clear! One more lesson from this – if you have a maths question, ask

Jim!

I really like the idea of choosing who you are going to be at work, choosing your attitude.

> What would the 'perfect performer' in your role look like?
>
> Is it someone who does everything you do, or is it someone who does things differently?

Is attitude nature or nurture?

In Mind Games, Annie Vernon talks about how elite athletes get into their optimum mental state to perform.

Here's what she writes:

"This book explores how each sportsperson will have become intimately acquainted with the contents of their head through trial and error, mistakes and reflection.

What we will discover in this book is that this process, or working out how to train mental skills such that each athlete finds their optimum, is entirely individual.

It's part nature, part nurture, part training."

In my experience, I would completely agree. It's part who you are (your personality and character traits you were born with), part how you were shaped and part – and I would believe this given the development role I do – training. I think you can train mental skills to help you find your optimum level.

All three elements play a part. And there's not much anyone can do with the nature bit (apart from nurture and train it).

I've always assumed my competitive nature was down to having a big brother I was constantly trying to keep up with. I'd always want to beat him- and anyone else! I remember struggling up hills as a kid on a family bike ride in Herefordshire, lagging behind so much that the others would have to slow down for me to catch up. Except when I would realise we were nearly at the end – at which point I would have a burst of energy and sprint-pedal towards home so I could be the first one back!

As an adult, I joined a gym at one point and was going several times a week. After a few months I mentioned that I was going in a conversation with my parents, and they asked why I was going. I said that I wanted to see if I could. They were baffled and asked what my end-goal was, whether to lose weight or for a specific goal. Again, it wasn't any of those things. Just going and trying to improve on my previous efforts – essentially competing with myself - was enough to motivate me every time. I didn't need to find any other stimulus or focus to push myself.

What drives you to work hard and try to improve? Is it competitiveness, a desire to be better, or do you need something more?

What can you add into the mix that helps?

Involuntary redundancy and ways to cope

When I was about 37 or 38, I had three young children and what felt like a big mortgage. Life was ticking along nicely and all was well. We were living in the south-west of England with plenty of friends but a long way from parents or any other family.

Then my job got made redundant. I choose my words here. I wasn't redundant. But the job I did was.

Whilst it wasn't a complete surprise, when it actually happened, it was still a nasty shock and left me feeling a bit out of control, uncertain and anxious.

One of the things that helped me was deciding I would aim to *be a role model employee whose job was being made redundant*. This meant:

- Choosing my response – I remember going to babysit for the evening at a friend's house and taking Stephen Covey's 7 Habits book, which I'd read just a few years before, to help me think about what I wanted
- Being brilliant at taking all the outplacement support that my employer offered, which was considerable
- Learning along the way – about what would happen and what I might want next
- Working hard to stay confident – reminding myself I was as good as I was the day before the announcement, backing myself to get a new job, telling myself I only needed one job
- Using the phrase "perfect is possible" to myself. Perfect is possible meaning the scenario where I got some redundancy money, had some time not working while still being paid, and getting a new job to start as soon as the existing one ended
- Keep working hard until the end in my job and not burning any bridges
- Being a role model to my colleagues and supporting those in a similar position – if this sounds cocky or generous it was neither really. It was designed to help me cope. I'm not sure if it helped them but I hope it did

I tell this story to show how an attitude and a strategy – in this case *"be a role model"* – can drive behaviour and get to a better outcome.

I've learnt since that many people get made redundant from roles. It's not personal. People may subsequently go through a month, two, three, six, a year or two before getting another job. Who knows? But eventually they do get another one. And however many or few jobs are around, you only need one.

Many, many people whose job is made redundant look back and with hindsight say it wasn't the worst thing that could have happened, and even that it was a good thing, because it prompted a positive change.

Like Jim, I've also been placed in a redundancy situation during my career. It's a tough experience to go through – and it can be a challenging subject to have conversations about. There is still plenty of stigma out there about letting people know you've been made redundant, particularly new employers. However, in the world we live in now, most people will experience a redundancy at some point in their careers. So many of us identify strongly with our work and use that identity as a marker for success and confidence. Losing that unexpectedly and suddenly can be very disorientating and demoralising.

One of the things I was struck by when it happened to me was just how many people reached out to me, either to offer support, share their stories, or to just listen. Jim was one of them, and his wise words and support were invaluable. I can tell you that he absolutely does live up to his aim of being a role model for others.

Have you ever been made redundant?

Who reached out to support you?

If you've ever had to make someone redundant, it can be an even harder topic to discuss. Most companies don't fly George Clooney in to deliver the awful news – it's usually down to the manager who knows that person or team best. You will have a strong sense of how the news is likely to affect those to be made redundant, both professionally and personally, but as 'the bad guy' you're not 'supposed' to be affected by it – the focus is rightly on supporting the person being made redundant. After all, "that's what you're paid the 'big bucks' for!"

Now, I don't know where these ideas about how I should feel came from, but I can guarantee you that they're not in any HR handbook! In fact, I don't think I've ever seen any rules about how you should feel when you make someone redundant – and I imagine that is because most people will feel terrible about it - which isn't really something you can write in your HR policies.

How 'should' you feel if you are forced to make a colleague redundant?

What kind of support would you need, and how would you want to respond to the situation?

The relative importance of knowledge, skills and attitude and which to work on

At the age of 32, I got a job in a training team, which was a career defining move.

I'd been invited to apply for a role by Damon, the Sales Training team manager. Early on Damon wrote on a flipchart the three words: Knowledge, Skills and Attitude. He told me that we train knowledge – like product knowledge – and that we could test what had been learned (and therefore evaluate how good our training had been). He told me that we also trained skills – like sales skills – but that this was harder to evaluate, especially in real customer situations. Finally he told me – as I recall - that we didn't train attitude.

Many years later I was becoming increasingly interested in the psychology of sales. Where I worked at that time, if you talked about the psychology of sales, the conversation would be about the interaction between buyer and seller. But for some reason I was much more interested in the performance psychology of the seller.

About then, I discovered that one of the new sales consultants that I had helped to run an induction programme for, was an elite level athlete. I took the opportunity to ask him if he had ever worked with a sports psychologist. He said he hadn't so I asked him if he would like to work with me. "I didn't know you were a sports psychologist, Jim", he replied. "I'm not", I said, "but I'm really interested to learn!".

And so he and I started talking about the mental side of his running. I should note that he was an experienced competitor and I didn't feel I was going to screw him up! I did have a bit of a scare though one lunchtime when I arranged to meet a local, newly qualified sports psyche working at a local college of further education. She told me I should have a written contract and all sorts of things in place in case our work made his running worse! I dashed back to work and urgently approached him and told him what she'd said. He laughed and was chilled. "Nah Jim, we're cool".

I think he quite enjoyed talking to me about his running. I was keen and interested and I'd like to think that the conversations helped him too.

In one of our first meetings – maybe the first – I wrote down

- Natural ability
- Health and fitness
- Mindset and attitude

and I asked him to put percentages against these three things in terms of their importance.

"At my level", he said (and that feels relevant) it's 5% natural ability ("We're all quick. That's how we got into sprinting"), 15% health and fitness ("We all train hard and look after ourselves") and 80% in your head ("At the moment the gun goes off").

Now in research terms, this is a sample size of one! But I was stunned, enthused and even more curious. There must be something in the mental thing, I thought.

My challenge became how to integrate what I knew, and what I was thinking, into my work. I created an opportunity by discussing with my internal client, the Regional Manager of Sales in Scotland and Northern Ireland, and his management team. They agreed I could do a slot at the next meeting of the 30 or so sales consultants and managers.

I was well prepared but felt like I was taking a risk. I was putting my credibility (what credibility I had) on the line and some of them were tough old, experienced, round-the-block sales consultants.

I remember clearly standing up at the front and after about 10 seconds of my presentation thinking "oh my goodness, what are you doing?" quickly followed by "you have to go on". That "you have to go on" was unplanned, simple and very effective self-talk.

And the risk paid off, the content landed, the comments were favourable and my confidence took a lift. It was one of several significant career and work developments at that time.

Whether it's trying to decipher what a rugby or tennis player has written on their wristbands or a post-match interviewer asking "What went through your mind during that moment?"; the opportunity of a glimpse into someone else's self-talk and attitude is always intriguing.

I'm pretty certain that back in humanity's cave-dwelling era, one of the questions from the fireside audience enraptured by the tale of a mighty hunt would have been "Were you scared?" And whether the answer was affirmative or not, it was probably followed by a "but then I remembered how hungry I was/you all are..."

We all use self-talk, whether it is positive or negative – and whether we listen to it or not! I'm sure we've all had moments like Jim, where we tell ourselves "you have to go on" in challenging situations.

*One of my favourite answers to this question was back in 2003, when the England rugby union side played New Zealand in Wellington a few months before their now-infamous World Cup win. England had two forwards sin-binned at a crucial period in the match, and were defending their try line against the New Zealand scrum. You never want to be a man down in the scrum, let alone two, yet England managed to hold out and win the game, an incredibly rare victory on All Blacks soil. After the game, the ever dour-looking captain and lock Martin Johnson was interviewed, and asked what was going through his mind during that infamous scrummage. He responded simply: "My spine."

What is your self-talk like, and how do you use it to your advantage?

Trusting the process (as an attitude)

By trust the process I mean, adopt a mindset which means you can approach a task in a prepared, relaxed and confident frame of mind. It means trusting that the process you have planned, and know, and have maybe used before, is one that will lead to a desirable outcome; whether that outcome is a goal, or a discovery or simply an end point.

In coaching I often use the process GROW or (T)GROW which stands for (Topic), Goal, (current) Reality, Options and Wrap up (or What next or Will (motivation)). It's a process that doesn't necessarily need to be used sequentially.

I once coached someone who had lodged an official grievance against what they believed to be the unfair, biased behaviour of a boss.

I told them about a time when my wife and I owned a house where we wanted to build an extension over our garage. When we told our neighbour about our plans they weren't happy because they thought it would affect the light onto their property. I felt the impact on them would be minimal.

We really felt we needed and wanted the extra space but I was equally keen not to fall out with my neighbour. I had seen that before in a previous house we had lived in where next-door neighbours living near us had fallen out terribly. They were an old couple and next door a young couple with a young baby. It got very petty, very awkward and quite unpleasant for everyone. The young couple had lots of friends round socialising and the old couple would often have their peace disturbed. On day the old man woke his young neighbours up in the early hours saying his wife was extremely ill and they must come and help. It wasn't true, and he just wanted them to experience how bad it was to be woken up. Relationships deteriorated further.

So my neighbour and I managed to talk about our situation and what we were both after. We managed to agree that I would apply, that he would object and we would see where the planning process took us.

Our first application was rejected, his objection was upheld. We were in the process of rethinking our plans to re-apply when events overtook us and we moved house, out of the city, to a small market town be closer to a better secondary school.

That was the story.

When I finished my coaching with the coachee, he told me that this story had really helped him with the grievance process. It helped him to focus on what he could control, to think more and not to react.

In high performance circles, where a team or individual has thoroughly prepared, 'trusting the process' enables them to choose a particular mindset, to relax, to deal with unhelpful nerves, and to perform to the best of their ability.

A few years back, having signed up with a local cat shelter and had a home inspection, I was expecting to wait a month or two before my name reached the top of the waiting list to adopt some kittens. One Friday morning a week or so after the inspection, I got a call at work asking me to come to a vet practice the following morning as there was a litter of five kittens needing homes immediately.

Having made a few emergency purchases, I arrived at the vets the next morning and was ushered into a back room by a charity volunteer to choose my kittens. I knew I could only take two, and they were all boys. So I sat on the floor, and a rather adventurous ginger tom kitten came to play with the toy I was flicking for him to chase. Great, I'd have him.

The second choice was tougher, but a little grey tabby intrigued me. He was clearly watching his ginger brother play, creeping nearer to get a better view and suss me out, but not getting involved. Eventually I chose him as I thought he was intelligent, and off home we went.

What I didn't quite realise was that having been found in the wild and then being in the back room of a vets rather than in a foster home meant that the kittens weren't very used to humans. Much as I wanted to cuddle them and stroke them to reassure them, on the first day I barely got close enough to touch them occasionally.

I won over the ginger kitten pretty quickly, but his brother was tougher. I couldn't take time off work, but every evening, I'd come home and sit on the kitchen floor and play with them, let them climb over me, and stroke them whenever they weren't looking. It was frustratingly slow in those early days, but at the same time I trusted that if I invested enough of the things I could control – time, play, and attention – they'd eventually let me stroke them. And in time, it did work.

Now I am constantly supervised by one or the other, they regularly demand attention, and I get ferociously meowed at if I don't go to bed when the tabby thinks I should (!) – so maybe I was too successful!

> When have you had to trust the process and focus on doing what was in your control? How did it work out for you?

"Hard work beats talent when talent doesn't work hard"

The heading to this story is a quote attributed to a US basketball coach called Tim Nokte. Like many good quotes it is both memorable and has meaning.

Of course if you are talented and work hard – as the coach implies – you stand a good chance of making the most of your talent.

I once heard Michael Johnson, the great American sprinter,

unequalled in the 200m and 400m interviewed on the radio. He was asked about his physical running style (he had a distinctive upright posture) and his mental toughness (for which he was renowned). Which was most important he was asked, the physical or mental? 'Both', he replied, 'both are important'.

The interviewer went on to ask a question near the end about whether there was a secret to his success? 'Yes, there is', he said. I could sense everyone listening to the radio at that moment leaning in to hear his answer a bit more clearly, just like I was.

He went on to explain that when he went to college (university) he joined the track and field (athletics) programme and that there were training sessions two or three times a week.

'I went to them all', he said.

And that was the 'secret of his success'. I took away from the interview his commitment to his sport, his hard work and his consistency.

When I was younger, I had the fortune (or misfortune) to be a member of my local Air Cadet squadron. It was unusually small and somewhat more relaxed than most squadrons would have been, which probably suited me very well. I enjoyed going twice a week and the opportunities – flying, gliding, target shooting, camps and so on – that came with being a member.

As a cadet, you not only had a series of exams and training to pass that offered status badges, you could also be promoted to leadership positions and help take charge of squadron activities and drill (marching). Because I showed up every week, followed the rules and passed my exams, I also found myself getting promoted regularly.

In a different squadron I might not have achieved as many promotions, but my commitment to showing up and working hard meant I was rewarded regularly.

I'm no Michael Johnson(!), but what I learned was as valuable for me as it was for him; by consistently showing up, working hard, and being committed to what you do, you can succeed.

What have you committed to in order to achieve success?

What did making that commitment teach you about yourself?

Enjoying yourself and having fun at work

We are all wired differently as a result of personality, upbringing, culture and values. I know I can be quite serious at times though also possess a sense of humour – of sorts.

To me work can be serious but not all the time. My memories of some of the best teams I have ever worked in include those of all the times we laughed together.

Enjoying yourself at work needn't be at the expense of doing a great job. Sometimes it even adds to the level of performance you are able to produce. Not 'larking around', but deliberately having a good time.

Years ago a colleague and I were working for two days with a very introverted team of technical experts. At the end of day one we were tired. Trying to generate responses and discussion had proved really hard work.

On the walk back to our hotel we talked about the day and our strategy for day two. We came up with two things:

1. Don't ask any questions of the whole group, especially open questions (not easy for us because this was our common practice)

2, Look to enjoy ourselves in the room and working together at the front of the group

Both tactics seemed to work well and not only was the room not full of tumbleweed silences but we had a good time as well – while absolutely looking to do our best work for the team. They seemed to enjoy it more too.

This might seem like a strange discovery – that seeking enjoyment can make everything better – but a discovery it is for many of us. Or is it just me?

My brother once worked for an organisation that moved across the country to a purpose-built office. He gleefully told me that he'd managed to organise a paper aeroplane competition in their new atrium, under the guise of getting people to enjoy their new environment and teambuilding.

Although he felt like he'd 'got away' with something that wasn't quite 'proper' work, it probably did exactly what he said it would – enabled his colleagues to connect, relax and enjoy themselves after the stress of the big move and settling into the new office.

At work, I often run discussion panels, virtual watercoolers and workshops that seem like quite light-hearted fun sessions. They're actually carefully designed to encourage colleagues to share their knowledge and wisdom and to start conversations across teams. The biggest challenge is persuading my colleagues that just because they're enjoying themselves, doesn't mean they're not also doing productive work!

Have you ever felt as if you couldn't be doing 'proper' productive work if you're enjoying yourself?

What makes you feel that way?

Even brain surgeons need downtime to reflect with colleagues, tell stories, and learn–

So what is stopping you enjoying yourself at work (even if only at the appropriate moment)?

Ways to get mentally ready

As mentioned earlier, I first started taking a proper interest in performance psychology in about 2001 when I was working with a colleague, now a friend, who was an accomplished sprinter. I hadn't initially realised how good he was but I learned that he was an international and Commonwealth games athlete.

As told earlier, I asked him if he'd ever worked with a sports psychologist? "No", he replied "but I would be interested to". "Would you like to work with me?" I asked, slightly hesitantly. "I didn't know you were a sports psychologist Jim", he said. "I'm not", I admitted "but I'm keen to learn!".

So the two of us began, fairly regularly, talking about the mental side of his running. He was already an experienced athlete in his late 20s and had lots of experience to draw on. We would talk about goals, and mindset, and how to think.

I remember our first conversation well and talking about two things.

Firstly, I asked him about 1. Natural ability 2. Health and fitness and 3. Mindset and attitude. I said if you had to apportion percentages to these three things to indicate their importance, what would you say?

He replied, "at my level", it's 5% natural ability ("we're all naturally quick – that's how we got into sprinting", 15% health and fitness ("we all look after ourselves and train hard") and 80% mindset and attitude ("at the moment the gun goes off it's all in your head").

I was pretty astounded. (I would point out to the reader that in research terms this is a sample size of one.)

Secondly, I asked him, how he gets himself mentally ready.

Within a minute or two I had written down 17 different things that he said he did to get ready. I was a keen learner and note taker and still have the piece of paper in the front leaf of a book (it's possible I double counted one in more than one category). I asked him where he learned these things and he said a mixture of places: from others, from just picking things up and from seeing what worked for him. Basically, word of mouth, copying and trial and error. Three tried and tested learning methods!

Most of all I was interested that he had *learned* them.

Later, in reading up on these things (in the Sports Psychology book where the piece of paper is kept), I came to see them as a mix of thought control strategies, emotional control strategies, behavioural strategies and attentional focus strategies.

17 things to get ready for a 10 second race!

In my rugby playing days, I was never the fittest member of the team. I certainly wasn't the fastest, and probably wasn't the strongest either. I was probably the most likely person to turn up – and to be honest, that can take you quite a long way in itself! The team I played for had a great atmosphere, but it had an ethos I hadn't come across anywhere else. Every player on that team was absolutely determined to push themselves to their limits. One of the stock phrases you'd hear at training, particularly during pre-season, was "train until you're sick."

At the time, none of us seemed to have any idea that this wasn't a healthy attitude. A few years later a group of us were talking and one former player explained they'd started a new sport that all their new fellow participants took seriously.

"Ah," I said. "Train until you're sick?"

"No." said my former teammate. "Apparently that's not a healthy attitude and other people find it quite shocking."

Being in our own little bubble had given us some really good mental strategies as a team – but also some really bad ones! Someone else's perspective on your approach can be really valuable.

Have you ever explained your mental preparation – whether for work, sport, or anything else – to an outsider to get their perspective?

How did that help you understand how you need to approach mental preparation for what you need to do?

---

2. BEHAVIOUR CHANGE

"The starting place for change is accepting oneself and taking interest in one's inner world."

ED DECI

"When you're finished changing, you're finished."

BENJAMIN FRANKLIN

Having worked for two and a half decades in training, coaching and consultancy roles it's not surprising that I have picked up a story or two about behaviour change.

Performing is to do something and if we are to grow and develop – and perform better – then it's our behaviour that is changing.

To me these stories that illustrate why, when and how behaviour changes can be both enlightening and very practical.

Paradigm shifts that change behaviour

Stephen Covey tells a great story – its visual nature makes it very memorable - about a paradigm shift early on in his book The 7 Habits of Highly Effective People. The story originated, as Covey states, from Frank Koch in Proceedings, the magazine of the Naval Institute.

"Two battleships assigned to the training squadron had been at sea on manoeuvres in heavy weather for several days. I was serving on the lead battleship and

was on watch on the bridge as night fell. The visibility was poor with patchy fog, so the captain remained on the bridge keeping an eye on all activities.

Shortly after dark, the lookout on the wing of the bridge reported, "Light, bearing on the starboard bow."

"Is it steady or moving astern?" the captain called out.

Lookout replied, "Steady, captain," which meant we were on a dangerous collision course with that ship.

The captain then called to the signalman, "Signal that ship: We are on a collision course, advise you change course 20 degrees."

Back came a signal, "Advisable for you to change course 20 degrees."

The captain said, "Send, I'm a captain, change course 20 degrees."

"I'm a seaman second class," came the reply. "You had better change course 20 degrees."

By that time, the captain was furious. He spat out, "Send, I'm a battleship. Change course 20 degrees."

Back came the flashing light, 'I'm a lighthouse."

We changed course."

A great story. And a wonderful example of how new information, or a shift, "puts the situation in a totally different light".

Often our existing perception of our current reality limits our thinking. If we can find or learn ways to get new knowledge or fresh perspective then our view is much richer.

Sometimes I receive emails at work that annoy me because I feel I haven't been properly consulted or someone has done something that doesn't seem to make sense. Often I start typing a response before re-reading and realising that I had not fully understood the message in the first place, and that it wasn't actually saying what I had thought at first.

Rather like the captain in the story Jim shared, I've learned that my first read of the situation isn't always the right one and I am much better to take a moment to ensure I fully understand what I'm being told.

Have you had to row back from your first response, either because you have not fully understood, emotion has clouded your perspective, or you didn't have the full picture? How difficult is it for you to 'change course'?

Has it helped you change how you respond, like I have learned to take a moment and re-read emails?

Strong emotions as a catalyst for change

Much of my work as a coach has been as a Performance Coach. Often I discuss at the outset with a client the scope of our work and typically the conclusion is that anything that can impact work is on the table to talk about and discuss - and that's a pretty wide scope that typically takes in all of a person's life outside of work.

One chap and I sat down to talk for the first time having first met when he was part of a cohort on a development programme. He was successful in his role, popular and identified by his employer as a future leader.

However he had a health challenge going on which he was ignoring and hadn't really talked about before. As we talked it became clear that his motives for change were compelling but he had lost control and didn't know where to start in climbing what had become a big mountain.

We both got a bit emotional in that conversation (a bit unusual for me at that time) and there were a few tears from each of us as we talked. It was challenging in different ways for both of us. For him to confront his feelings and for me to check he was ok and keep managing the coaching process.

As we continued to talk he became clearer and clearer that not only did he want to do something, but we developed a plan that he really wanted to do.

It's pretty obvious but uncovering the reason for doing something different – the why – can be a pretty important, if not the most important, step.

His why was very personal. His health had the very real prospect of negatively impacting others close to him. Suddenly he had a why, and a plan, and a first step.

It can be really easy to avoid acknowledging our emotions when things change, especially when things aren't going well. I worked with someone once who, when placed into a redundancy process, admitted to feeling predominantly relieved. Despite enjoying parts of their job, various challenges and stresses had combined to make her dread what each day would bring, and she would often find herself crying on the train to work each morning.

Instead of acknowledging that the problems with her job were so deep-rooted that her unhappiness and stress could only be resolved by finding a new role, she tried to avoid confronting those emotions, leading to the enormous relief when forces outside her control changed the situation for her. If she'd acknowledged the unhappiness earlier and started looking for a new role, she might have both relieved some of the pressure on herself and avoided the stress of redundancy.

I've often found myself talking to friends and colleagues about how to decide when it is the right time to look for your next job. One of the points that often comes up is that the tipping point, the place you draw the line, is much clearer in retrospect than at the time. In fact, if someone was to tell you at the time "that was the line, you've just stepped over it" you'd probably tell them that you thought someone had dropped some chalk, as it looked like a pretty faint line to you.

When was the last time you examined your feelings and emotions about a particular situation, and how did they help guide you in moving forwards?

Being challenged to a change in behaviour through a new realisation

Sometimes in teams, experienced team members are required to contribute more than just their technical expertise. The culture requires that they bring more than that. I enjoyed the example given by Gareth Thomas in the documentary series Slammed, about Welsh rugby in the early 2000s.

Wales had a new coach, the New Zealander Steve Hansen. He came into his role feeling that the standards of fitness and professionalism were not at the necessary level.

Thomas recalls: "I liked what he brought but mate, he was harder on me than anyone else."

"There came a time where Steve was kind of like saying to me "mate, how many caps have you got? Like how many times have you played for Wales?" And I don't know exactly at the time maybe 50 odd, something like that.

And he was like "What, you're a 50 cap player, and we have a team meeting and you sit at the back of the room and you say f*$% all and you do not contribute, to anything". And he was like "if you're a 50 cap player, and that's all you're bringing to the table, then mate, I don't want you at my table. You're worthless to me"."

Hansen went on to tell Thomas that whether he liked it or not the rest of the team saw him as a leader and was the guy they looked to. He said to him I need you to be the best professional you can be and this team needs you to be that.

Thomas went on to win 100 caps for his country.

It's a great lesson for many leaders and the more senior members of teams (and anyone else). What do you contribute? What can you bring?". If no-one has asked you, then you can always ask yourself.

I can sometimes be a bit chatty, particularly in groups that I'm comfortable in and where I believe my contribution can add value. Often this is helpful, particularly in more senior roles or where people are being quiet. However, I also have to keep in mind that often if I'm talking or especially if I'm talking a lot, someone else isn't. I am very mindful to try and bring others into the conversation if they haven't had the chance to contribute, whilst also not wanting to pressure anyone who doesn't feel very comfortable speaking in front of the group.

I've also learned that I should think about the balance of my contributions. Am I always being critical or only suggesting improvements? What have I said that is positive or helpful to balance that out?

How do you recognise when you need to speak up or lead the discussion, and also when you need to encourage others to speak up and be heard?

What helps you encourage others to speak if they aren't comfortable, and how do you find a way to make yourself heard if you aren't comfortable speaking up?

And how do you ensure that your contribution is helpful?

Using what's available around you - your environment - to create a behaviour change

New habits can be hard to create – or old habits can be hard to shake – especially if they're linked to natural behaviour.

I once worked with a colleague, Emma, jointly running a presentation skills course. She was a fast talker, and a problem was that often she was too quick for her audience when presenting. They didn't have time to assimilate what she was saying!

She explained how people had told her to slow down in her speed of delivery, but although she had tried, she could never do it, at least not without then stumbling over her thoughts and words as a result, and losing her flow.

But she had managed to find a solution by always having a glass of water with her. She learned to take a sip of water, to create the pauses, to allow the audience a breather to think. She still delivered her words as fast, but with pauses.

I love this example of behaviour change and using the environment to help you.

It's a bit like the ex-colleague in Birmingham who used to make his lunchtime sandwiches the night before and freeze them. That way he had to wait until lunchtime to eat them, by which time they had defrosted, rather than eating them half way through the morning!

Setting up the environment can help create new behaviour and habits.

We all had to use what was around us during lockdown over the past few years. Prior to the pandemic, I had started using Instagram and at some point, decided to post a photo a day. Initially it was to gauge whether my photos of the places I'd travelled to and wildlife were good enough to sell, and after a while, I realised it was good discipline to edit a photo a day as it meant I actually got round to photo editing!

A few months before lockdown I'd splashed out on a long-desired macro lens for my camera, ideal for close-ups of bees, insects and flowers. Being lucky enough to have a garden meant that when I couldn't go anywhere, I still had daily subjects for photography, especially in summer. Even today, my camera is sitting next to me, macro lens attached, and if I see a butterfly going past or the light fall on the flowers just right, I'll be out in the garden snapping away. Seeing the garden in this new and ever-changing way has meant I haven't missed the trips away and to see family that were a feature of pre-Covid life in quite the same way. There will always be a new flower or another butterfly in the garden if I go out and look for them, and I can quite happily sit and watch the bees buzz through the flowers for ages.

> How have you used what's around you over the last few years
> to mitigate and solve problems?
>
> What have you learned from those changes?

Three ways to create habits

I read more, and hear more talk, about what high performance habits are, rather than how to create them.

A few years ago I ran a session for a customer business on performance nutrition. Not being a qualified nutritionist, but being a qualified coach, I ran a session based on why good nutrition is important for performance, what good nutrition is at a common sense level, about the challenges of eating well in the 21st century - which is not easy - and about doing what you know.

I ran the session 3 times in a day for groups of about 15-20 people.

At the end of one session one middle aged chap was persistent that the session hadn't told him *how* to eat well. I was frustrated because I felt that the session I had run was exactly that! I let the frustration live with me for a while, recalling it occasionally when my mind drifted.

Eventually it prompted me to go away and look online for articles about habit creation and I found one in particular that I found useful. It highlighted three things:

1. Use goals to help you – so set goals about the outcome but also about the habit i.e. how often you would do the thing
2. Engage the support of others to help you create the habit. This could be family, friends or colleagues who can play a role in the

habit creation

3. Set your environment up to help with the habit creation. Leave physical reminders in place or try and remove things getting in the way. Create a new habit on the back of an existing one

These three things are simple, memorable and practical. Any of the three are helpful but done together they are particularly useful.

And it was my frustration that led to this learning. Frustration + Proactivity = Learning + Solutions

One of the challenges of the modern world that Jim has already mentioned is the deluge of messages telling us what to watch, consume, think (depending on your bubble) and what is good and bad. On the whole, we trust these messages because they tend to be self-reinforcing; I enjoyed that show, I liked this food I saw advertised, I believe this about the government's actions, and I don't think we should - as a society - do that. When we constantly hear these messages, being confronted with a situation where we're told to not only buck the trend and consider what messages are right for us, but that we have to make an active choice about what is right for us, can be very challenging.

Often, if you're advising people to buck the trend and question which messages are right for them, it can be very disorienting. Choosing your own message, without the confirmation from the wider world that is correct, or against conflicting messages, can cause us to question ourselves and seek a clearer direction. "If you want me to not do what I did before, tell me what I should do!"

I was once talking to an online acquaintance in a discussion forum. They had asked a question about a scenario I had experienced and I sent them a message outlining the options available to them, and what they needed to look into for each of those options. They were finding the situation very difficult and stressful, and made it clear that they just wanted someone else to tell them exactly what to do and how to do it – or ideally, do it for them. That wasn't something I could do, and I had to tell them that.

It can be challenging to be asked for direction like this when you know it isn't appropriate to give it. Being in this position is a bit of a Catch-22 – you know that if you do as the person is asking and make choices for them, you are likely to pick the wrong option, because you don't know them or their context well enough to know what is right. But if you tell them to make their own choice, they will feel let down because the situation itself is making them feel out of control.

Jim's choice in this situation is really valuable; he hasn't told the frustrated individual what to do, nor is he going to tell anyone else. But he has found a way to give his audience who are making difficult choices some practical tools to help them make their choices successful, whatever option they take.

> How do you respond when someone asks you for something you can't give them?

Getting started on something when you're stuck – just start!

A few weeks into my first training job my manager, Damon, sent me on a presentation skills course. I think he kindly told me it was a standard course that all trainers in his team had been on. In reality I think he thought I really needed some help, and I did.

On the course I told the trainer that I had bought a book in which to start writing quotes, which I liked, that I could use in presentations. The trainer thought that was a great idea. However, I explained to him, I couldn't decide whether to write the quotes in the book by author or by subject matter.

"How many have you written in so far?" he asked.

"None", I replied, "because I can't decide".

"If I was you", he said, leaning closer, "I would just start writing them".

There are many reasons why we don't start, or put things off - procrastination, wanting something to be perfect and fearing that it might not be. Often starting IS the hardest part so sometimes it's best just to start.

Even though I "know this", I still find myself needing to remember it and to do it. Some lessons are slow to learn or only infrequently applied. I definitely have applied this learning since, though not always as quickly as I might have.

Just like Jim, I often find it hard to get started on things. The longer I leave it, the larger the thing looms over me – and it's amazing what you find yourself spending time on when there is something looming! Yet usually when I start the thing, it's either less painful than I thought, a relief to have done, and sometimes even – like this - very enjoyable to do!

Sitting down to write this has taken me several weeks – and even since I started a few hours ago, I've put the bins out, turned the football on (I'm not a fan of football, but it's the women's Euro 2022 final so I'm looking at the TV occasionally), fed the cats, had a snack, and made another 3 trips out to the bin with things I'd forgotten to put in it. However, I'm not only enjoying sitting and writing – and using those pauses to think about what I might write next and reflect on what I've written already – but I'm also dreading the thought of pausing part way through a first effort and having the thought of finishing this still looming!

How often do you struggle to get started on things?

What can you use to help you get started, and how do you feel when you finally achieve something that you've been struggling to focus on?

Do you have any mitigation strategies that help you avoid getting caught in procrastination?

And are there times when waiting to get started helps you to order your thoughts, and perform better once you do actually begin?

3 PERSONALITY

"Everything that irritates us about others can lead us to an understanding of ourselves."

JUNG

"The shoe that fits one person pinches another; there is no recipe for living that suits all cases."

JUNG

We are all different is a great truism. In essence, the stories in this section illustrate this in their different ways.

In many ways, our personality is the very essence of what we bring to our performance and our work.

Developing self-awareness, and understanding how others are different to you, is continually fascinating and valuable.

The value of working with someone different to you

I know I can easily get stuck in my ways. Also I can be narrow in my thinking, so that when things change I can fail to think of new alternative scenarios, my mind unconsciously locked into the original plan.

I know too that one of my challenges is starting something, but once I get going I can be both patient and persistent.

I can tread carefully too. It can take me a lot of effort to take what feels like a leap.

As a small example of difference, back in 1998 I was struggling to learn how to use this technology thing called the internet. It was all new and I was very cautious in my navigating. Fortunately I was sat in an office next to David Underwood and he was an explorer. An Internet Explorer.

He seemed happy to just click on things and see what happened (where I was worried I would do something bad and crash the company mainframe). By watching and copying him I learned so much.

Another example involved me introducing a colleague, Lou, to a partner in a small business I was consulting with. The business was struggling and the relationship between the two partners was deteriorating. I had invited my colleague to help because of his financial expertise.

However after introducing the partner and my colleague, the first 10 minutes were *all* about empathy and relationship building. I was all ready to get quickly into a conversation about numbers but my naturally empathetic colleague – who himself had run a struggling business previously – knew better. It was so appropriate and helped them form the foundation for a very constructive conversation where it was obvious that my colleague really cared.

I cared to but wasn't capable at the time of expressing it in that way.

An appreciation of others who are different to you, like David and Lou who are different to me - acknowledging and benefitting from their strengths (hopefully in a mutual way) - is often a good way to go.

If you're reading this book, you're probably, like Jim, interested in what makes people tick. You might be interested in coaching too. One of the biggest challenges of coaching is knowing when to let someone discover the answer on their own, and when to prompt them more directly towards it.

In this case, Jim was told the next step pretty directly by his manager – who had recognised that Jim needed a direct prompt. Watching someone take their next step, either prompted or through their own realisation, is a wonderful and fulfilling thing to see.

How do you prompt the people around you to explore their next step?

How do you tell the difference between someone who needs an indirect prompt to find their own answer, and someone who needs a stronger nudge?

Different people and personalities have different targets and aspirations

Being a father of three gives the opportunity, close at hand, to observe differences in personality, which are wide and apparent very early on.

As an example, two of my children had very different, natural, responses to the targets on their school reports. For a while the reports contained a list of the different subjects with two columns next to them: Target Grade and Aspirational Grade.

One of my children used to look at the Aspirational Grade column. This was the grade that the teachers felt was just about possible - achievable with hard work and if all went well.

Another of my children was focused solely on the Target Grade column. This grade was what the teachers felt was a more likely grade to make as a target. When I pointed out the Aspirational Grade column to this child I was told "yes Dad, but this is my target" (pointing at the Target Grade column).

Two different personalities at play I think! I don't feel that there is a right or wrong here. Working hard can be more important than what specific goal or target you have. Years later I met a chap who had been, variously, a child actor, a business manager and a professional poker player. He said his acting agent had given the advice: "It doesn't matter what you do until you are 30, as long as you do something".

If you are part of a team it often helps to be aware of the different starting points that people have. Some will be naturally focused on the target, and some on what's possible beyond it. Both can work.

I once worked in a place that used the bell-curve principle for its annual performance reviews. There were five grades of achievement, two positive, one neutral/average, and two negative. In practice, however, the rule about the top positive grade was that only one or two people in the whole organisation were allowed to achieve it. It was aspirational, but in practice impossible to achieve and therefore both pointless and discouraging for staff working their hardest.

Fortunately the system was reformed after I'd been there a little while and the impossible grade was removed. Suddenly the organisation had a lot more high performers!

What are your aspirations?

Are they realistic?

How different should aspirations be from pragmatic targets and goals?

Staying open to new possibilities and chance

A few years ago two colleagues and I were working with a customer at a small conference in a largish hotel. Living in different parts of the country we all travelled separately in our own cars and had arranged to meet early at the venue.

We planned to arrive early but me being me I arrived even earlier. I parked and went into the venue to look around. From the reception area I found my way to the large main room where the conference would take place and where staff were still setting up for the day.

I went back to my car to get my things and soon my two colleagues arrived at the same time. As I joined them walking into the hotel they were already deep in conversation. Walking into reception they were still chatting away and they simply walked straight on, past the turning to the room that I knew we were meant to be in.

Because we were still early, and they were so deep in conversation, I resisted the obvious urge to say something, and decided instead to just follow them, out of curiosity!

Part of the customer branding for the conference that day emphasised a thick red line in their company logo, which they were using very overtly to deliver a message in their latest TV marketing campaign. As part of our session we were also planning to deliberately use a thick red line in an exercise to make a learning point.

As my colleagues walked down a hotel corridor, one of them, who had volunteered to buy and bring some thick red marker pens for us to use, shared that he hadn't managed to get any over the weekend (he'd run out of time or couldn't find what we needed – it must have been pre-Amazon days!). We all said no matter, and we would improvise something.

After what seemed like 5 minutes of wandering the hotel corridors, with occasional stops at junctions for the two of them to, seemingly randomly, choose which way to go, we came to a larger open area where various people were setting up small exhibitions and stalls. It turned out that the hotel was hosting a large teachers' conference that day too.

And one of the stalls had the biggest display of coloured marker pens that I've ever seen.

My colleague quickly blagged a large box of red ones and we continued on our way.

Even though I'd arrived first, and early, my personality would have taken me straight to the room, with minimal exploring. I loved the serendipity of finding the teachers' conference and the pens. But exploring in that way, for me, would have to be a conscious effort.

Towards the end of the year I spent in New Zealand, aged 18, I decided to leave my job and spend my last few weeks before heading home driving around the North Island, seeing the sights.

One of the weeks took me up to the top of the island, Northland, and I decided to head for the northernmost town, Kaitaia. North of Kaitaia is a spit of land stretching north for a hundred miles or so, with 'Ninety-Mile-Beach' on the west shore, and Cape Reinga, a lighthouse marking the sacred spot where the Tasman Sea meets the Pacific Ocean. According to

Māori legend, the spirits of the dead leap into the water from an ancient Pohutakawa tree at the Cape, and journey to their ancestral homeland of Hawaiki.

I decided on the afternoon of arriving to Kaitaia that I'd head up to Cape Reinga, hoping that the trip wouldn't take too long as it was winter and would be dark in the late afternoon. Unfortunately I didn't leave enough time, and having made some excursions off the main road to spend time on Ninety Mile Beach, decided to turn round and head home.

At one point, admiring the scenery, I decided to pull the car over and take a picture. Unfortunately what had looked like a safe verge turned out to be a ditch, and my ancient Toyota got stuck. On a deserted road with no mobile phone (and likely no coverage if I had had one), I tried but couldn't get the car out.

In what turned out to be a huge stroke of luck, a local drove past, stopped, and tried to pull me out. I had a thin rope in the boot but it snapped as soon as it took the force of the tow. Fortunately there was a donkey in a nearby field watching proceedings – probably with great amusement. The donkey was tied up with a sturdy-looking rope, so I used my snapped rope to tie it up, and borrowed the donkey rope. The driver helping me was surprised at my gumption, but we had another go. With a bit of wheel spinning, we managed to get my car out and I offered my rescuer some cash to buy their first jug of beer at the pub as they were on their way to town. I swapped the ropes back, patted the donkey, and headed back to town for the night.

Serendipity? Absolutely! Not only was I in enormous luck to have someone pass who could stop and help, but having a donkey tied up right there with a rope that was strong enough to tow me out was so fortuitous that you couldn't have designed the scenario any better – save not going into the ditch in the first place.

Would my rescuer - or anyone else - have considered swapping the ropes? Maybe not, and possibly rightly as if the donkey rope had broken it would have been most unfair on its owner given that my thin rope probably wouldn't have held the donkey there long-term.

When have you made a change or taken a decision that solved your problem, even if unintentionally?

Why did you choose that option?

Not getting too settled and being ready for change - again

I think the idea of 'waiting for a change to settle' in work and 'having a period of stability' are just about old hat. That change is here to stay is nothing new.

I once worked in a team of eight where half the roles got made redundant. As it happens, we were made up of four consultants and four senior consultants and the senior roles were staying. One of my consultant colleagues who, like me, was going, was reasonably ok with the situation. He had worked for the business for a long time and the prospect of a largish redundancy payment helped soften the blow – exactly as is intended.

However, having come to terms with leaving, one of the senior consultants then applied for, and got, a different role in the business, meaning my colleague's redundancy was no longer on the table. He had to stay.

After a short period of readjustment, he got his head around staying. After all, he hadn't wanted to leave in the first place.

It's no wonder "Who moved my cheese?" is such a popular read. Keep your shoes ready.

As I've got older and more experienced in my career, I've started to notice when I react badly to change. When I was younger all change was exciting and an opportunity to learn something new. I've sometimes been surprised to discover my own resistance to – for example – a new piece of business software.

I've always found I've had good reasons for the resistance – maybe the new software requires me to work in a way that is counter-intuitive to what I've found most helpful in the past. Maybe because it's new it feels intimidating if I don't know how to work it. Maybe too many things are changing too quickly for me to feel confident that I have mastered them?

How have you noticed your attitude to change has shifted with time?

Is change easier or harder the more of it you experience?

What would help you find change easier?

Appreciating what each of us brings to the journey

I read a great book a few years ago which taught me what different things people bring in times of change and uncertainty and enabled me to appreciate those things.

It was by Linda Kirby and Nancy Barger and it told the story of the early pioneers making their way across the USA on the Oregon Trail. It included diary extracts of the people who were there.

The story began with the early settlers on the east coast, who were trying to farm in unknown conditions and grow enough food to last them through the harsh winters. Life was tough.

Gradually one or two explores were heading west and coming back with great stories of beautiful lands where resources were plentiful and crops would grow well. Their enthusiasm and the vision they created was compelling and many were tempted to head west.

However, many other people, despite the harshness of their current environment, didn't want to leave what they knew. They were convinced that next year's crop would be better and they would be ok.

Eventually though, tempted by the tales of a better life, families and groups began to pack their belongings into wagons and head off.

Initially, some of them tried to take everything they owned with them, but as they set out they soon realised they couldn't carry all their possessions. The wagons were too heavy, and they had to ditch some things that were important to them in the past, that might not be needed in the future.

It turned out that some of the rough maps they had been provided with were pretty inadequate, some of the stories they had heard were untrue, and they came across lots of unexpected challenges and difficulties.

Some of the early enthusiasm of the get-up-and-goers began to fade. But new skills came to the fore too. The resourceful found ways to adapt.

After weeks and months they came to their toughest test, the Rocky Mountains. Now people had to ditch some of the things that were most precious to them to lighten their load. Where they had previously had to unload Grandma's old rocking chair, now they had to get rid of her rolling pin too.

And it was at this point, when some people were giving up – and even talking of returning east - that some of those who were most reluctant to leave in the first place came forward with their steady energy to keep going. They had come this far, and they weren't in favour of going back.

And finally, even as they began to settle in the west, some people were beginning to look out to sea at where they could go next.

We all bring different things at different times to changes and transitions – vision, storytelling, energy, enthusiasm, cautiousness, resourcefulness, practicality, determination... Appreciating each other in a team or group can be an enormous asset.

I first heard this story from Jim, and it has stuck with me as a really valuable way of understanding that not everyone adopts change – or adds value – at the same time. Instead of getting frustrated that others can't understand my enthusiasm for something new, I try to bear in mind that they may not be enthusiastic until further down the line. If they are critical, I try to understand their perspective and think about what their questions are helping me to achieve and why they are asking them.

Back in my rugby playing days, I organised a couple of end of season tours over the May bank holidays. These were the highlight of the season for many of the team, and we tended to go to a European city or town, enjoy the local beer and sights, and play a match against a local team who would inevitably be taking the contest far more seriously than the hungover shambles of a side that we would field.

Leading the tours could be quite stressful, if only because arranging food, drinks and entertainment for 20+ women in a foreign city required a lot of planning and organisation. I would usually rope in a few teammates to help with the planning and admin, and there were a number of tour roles that players took on that were – at times – helpful.

What I hadn't expected was that whenever things were a little chaotic – perhaps we were trying to navigate our way out of a busy station none of us had set foot in before, or arranging things with our opponents when we arrived at a game, or even dealing with challenges that cropped up; - someone would always step up to either manage the situation or help me out. From the most junior to the players who hadn't even wanted to go to that city, someone would be shepherding us through a station or tidying up the changing room or negotiating a table for 25. Whilst leading tour was an exhausting job, having people step up unexpectedly - and often before you even knew you needed them - made a huge difference to it being a positive experience for everyone.

When have you experienced people bringing different things to a change or challenge?

How did others surprise you with their response when the group were facing a tough time?

What did you learn from the different approaches of others?

How we naturally care for other people in different ways

People care in different ways. Some people want to care by doing practical things. And if there's nothing they can do they can feel helpless.

Others want to care by putting their arm around someone, or being there for them. They might get on to practicalities second.

I was once on a bike ride of several hours one morning with five or six friends. We were all in our 40s and were 'training' (I use the word loosely) for a planned week's bike ride from Biarritz to Perpignan taking on some of the larger, classic Pyrenean climbs along the way.

It was a very hot early spring day. One of the group, the organiser of the overseas trip, was a GP. He was just back from a family holiday on a long-haul flight and perhaps had a bit of a cold. He had also been a bit stressed at work of late and was wondering what workload he would be returning to. He was also carrying quite a bit of extra weight. So he was keen to come out that day to get a bit fitter, despite being under the weather.

We cycled for a few hours, up and down some Welsh hills, villages and countryside, before descending into the Wye valley. We had started off crossing over the River Severn in England, near Bristol, having cycled over the old Severn Bridge toll road (as it was then).

As we reached the bottom of our descent, we turned right onto a more main road to go past the ruin of Tintern Abbey and up a long drag, when the doctor stopped and asked if anyone had a mobile phone. He had got off his bike and was moving to sit on the pavement, against a wall, in the shade.

A phone was passed to him from a pocket or saddle bag and he calmly explained to us that he thought he might be having a heart attack. He paused briefly before saying yes, he was going to call an ambulance. A paramedic car arrived very quickly and soon decided that he had/was having a heart attack and called a bigger ambulance to take him to hospital.

The rest of us were all a bit shocked but I remember two or three of us, including me, discussing how we were going to get his bike back home. What a pity, we said, that it hadn't happened on our side of the bridge, so he could be taken to a hospital in Bristol, and no-one would have to pay the toll to come over the bridge in their car to collect the bike. How inconvenient.

Then one of the group asked who was going to go with the GP friend in the ambulance to the hospital? Which one of us? The thought hadn't even occurred to me. I was still working on the bike problem. And I wasn't thinking about the care of the patient. Doh!

In the end I was the one who went with him, and seeing him in the ambulance, sweating, with an oxygen mask on, did shock me, causing my more caring, human side to kick in. It was/is there all along but it's not always on the surface!

Since then I've learned to listen to it a lot more. Putting myself in other people's shoes is in many ways a learned behaviour, but it can be done.

Over the years, I've come to really appreciate the different ways people around me show that they care for me, even if it's not quite what I'd ask for at the time. Some people – like Jim – are very pragmatic and focused on problem-solving. Sometimes that is perfect and absolutely what I need. Sometimes people show they care by listening, or by offering sympathy. And sometimes it's by getting me involved in something, which is generally a good idea.

Many years ago I was asked to arrange something for my rugby team after I had stopped playing, and I probably should have turned down the request. It didn't go as smoothly as I'd hoped as I was unwell at the time, and it turned out I'd been asked because it had been seen as an opportunity for me to stay involved with the team, rather than because no-one else could do it. If I'd known that when I was asked, I would have explained that that I probably was a bit too unwell to take it on if someone else could manage it. Fortunately, things worked out in the end, and I appreciated the sentiment that had prompted the request – it had been thoughtful and caring.

How do people show you that they care?

How do you find ways to appreciate it?

And how do you find yourself showing how you care for others?

Many of us are natural planners... and many are not!

I had a boss once, now a friend – he used to be a colleague but got promoted to team manager – whose idea of a plan was that it was a starting point, rather than something to necessarily follow.

Everyone on the Business Consultancy team he led valued being in the team and was interested in development and improvement. We used to have regular team meetings, often all day, and usually once a month or so.

Under his leadership the meetings rarely had a fixed agenda, though everyone understood that there would be a mixture of discussing the topics of the day, challenges anyone was facing in their work and sharing what we were learning from our customer work or other development activity.

Then one day, out of the blue, he sent an agenda round in advance. It had timings on it and everything. It was so out of character that we were shocked and joked with one another about whether he was ok or had been on a course.

When we gathered on the day I had printed out a copy of the agenda (me being me) but the first thing he said was, "I know I shared an agenda for today, but something else has come up, so we will be focusing on that first, and not using the agenda after all".

Normal service had been resumed. To our relief.

I'm the natural planner by the way, who puts a plan together with the idea of following it to get to where I want to get to. But I know that with that focus I can get narrow and potentially miss opportunities. I try and stay more open minded to possibilities and see the value that others bring who are naturally like that.

Like Jim's former boss, I can be a bit impromptu and chafe a bit at writing down plans and following instructions if I think there is a better way. When I first graduated, I took a job as a trainee Librarian at a very small university. I was a bit of a general dogsbody and spent most of my time on the issue desk, but was also nominally in charge of the reserve shelves behind the front counter, where reserved books would wait to be collected.

Although I knew the full alphabetical order of shelving by author, in particular for the tricky 'Mac/Mc' authors, I didn't find it particularly logical to use. Because I was in charge of the reserve shelves, I figured it would be fine to shelve those particular books in the way that made most sense to me.

After a few weeks of doing this, I overheard a colleague grumble in exasperation about the person putting reserved books in the wrong order. I explained that I'd done that as it made more sense to me.

My colleague pointed out – fairly patiently in the circumstances – that that was all very well, but I wasn't always there to retrieve the books and no-one else knew I wasn't following the standard rules, so they were struggling to find what they were looking for. I quickly rearranged the books correctly and from then on, shelved them according to the rules.

In this way, I'm the opposite to Jim – whilst he tries to stay open-minded about the possibilities of opportunities outside the plan, sometimes I have to stay open-minded to rules being there for a reason, even if they aren't immediately logical to me.

Are you a planner or a bit more spontaneous?

Do you like to follow your own ideas or stick to the tried and tested because it works?

How does that affect the people around you?

And could you be more open to doing things differently if that makes them better?

Planned or overly structured? There are times to be flexible and roll with it

Another member of that same Business Consultancy team was even more organised and timely than me. If a meeting was due to finish and we were still talking, he would be packing up his things ready to go and might well leave anyway at the set time.

The joke was that he was planning to be more spontaneous, and had set a date to start.

Being like that had its upsides. He was very efficient and you knew where you stood with him. I always felt it was a shame when he seemed to dash off, without taking part in the post meeting team chat and small talk.

It also got him in trouble once. At a sales conference a learning task was set with small groups each given a video camera and instructions for filming particular content. Each group then had a set, limited time in an editing room. When the group in front of his ran over their time he wasn't happy. He banged on the door, opened it and told the group inside, in no uncertain terms, that their time was up and to clear off. Now it was the turn of the Sales Director, who was a member of the group inside, to not be happy.

Structure has a place but there are times to be flexible.

In my old rugby team, for a while I was in charge of taking training apologies and passing them onto the coaches. The coaches – volunteers – wanted to know as far as possible in advance how many people would attend training, so that they could plan the session effectively. I had a job at the time that never required me to stay late, so I felt that being able to send apologies well in advance was pretty reasonable.

Some of my teammates were solicitors, barristers, accountants, or worked in finance in the City of London. They all trained incredibly hard as well as working hard, and several of them would walk off the pitch on a Sunday afternoon and open their laptops and Blackberries to catch up on the progress of a critical deal or project. Naturally, they often couldn't get to a weekday evening training session if they got stuck in the office dealing with something urgent.

This was pretty frustrating for the coaches – when you only have half the numbers you expected it's not easy to run a planned session. It took me several years to find myself in roles and work environments where I could understand why my teammates would have had no choice but to miss training despite their best intentions.

Regardless of whether someone is struggling to be flexible or to be structured, it can be really easy to judge what appear to be choices without understanding the full context – whether it is Jim's former colleague who couldn't be spontaneous, or my former teammates who had no choice but to be flexible for their jobs.

How do you view the people around you and the choices they seem to be making about being spontaneous or structured?

How well do you understand their context?

Be very careful of closed thinking that narrows possibilities

My personality means I can be very closed.

A few years ago I had an acute period of lack of sleep. After two or three what felt like literally sleepless nights I went to see my GP. We talked through options, including sleeping pills, but having chatted it through with him I felt reassured and decided to wait in the hope that it settled down. And sure enough my sleeping soon settled down to normal.

Many years later I went to see the same GP about some hay-fever related asthma I get. I wanted to just check if anything had changed in my condition or medication.

I sat in a chair next to the doctor's desk as he went to the back of his room to get the small bit of apparatus for me to blow into to test my lung capacity. As he did so I happened to look to my right, to his computer screen on the far side of his desk, and my eyes zeroed in on the word 'anxiety'.

"Oh my goodness", I thought, "he's left the previous patient's notes up on his screen. How unprofessional".

As I blew into the apparatus I was wondering if I should say something to him but instead, as he turned to put the apparatus back in the cupboard, I couldn't help but immediately turn round to have another look at the screen.

And, of course, they were my notes I was reading all along. It's just that I'd never considered myself to have ever had anxiety, but there it was in black and white – his diagnosis.

This closed thinking - not exploring other possibilities - is a trait. I'm sometimes aware of it in work and I see it in others too. And I also see and appreciate flexibility and openness in others. I know that sometimes when they are being creative, I need to keep quiet, or not stop their flow, or simply encourage them.

Sometimes my closedness can be like a handbrake to others. Handbrakes are incredibly useful things of course, but not when you're trying to go somewhere and someone is sitting applying the handbrake all the time.

I see practical people operating the handbrake in meetings. They do it when others are creating and idea generating, and they say things like "that would never work" or "how would that work in practice". They put the brakes on! There's a time for narrowing possibilities but that time is not all the time.

I have a rather similar story to Jim's; I was visiting a chiropractor recently and talked about some of the stresses I was experiencing at that time. At the end of the session, the chiropractor made some notes and voiced them out loud, saying; "Some anxiety."

I was pretty surprised, as I'd interpreted what I'd mentioned as stress rather than anxiety. Like Jim, the idea of being anxious hadn't really crossed my mind. I was initially a little frustrated – the pronouncement seemed rather judgemental and didn't reflect my own take on the situation. Was I being closed to the idea that I was anxious? Quite possibly.

It made me think about interpretation; if I don't think I'm anxious but other people do, am I correct but need to work on how I express myself, or does their perception override mine and I need to think outside my own closed perspective?

I was on a call a few weeks ago, with a colleague onscreen and a couple of other people in the room alongside her that I couldn't see, and we discussed various different issues and problems. After the call, I said to my colleague that I'd felt some of the people in the room were a little apprehensive and concerned about a couple of issues. My colleague said that being in the room with them, she'd felt that they were just taking on board information about the issues for the first time, and didn't have any strong feelings about them.

In this case, not seeing the full context of the situation – the body language of the participants – meant that my interpretation of their reactions was wrong. My expectation that I'd be able to understand everything without seeing what was happening was perhaps a little too closed!

> Have you ever experienced your reading of the situation being totally different to someone else's perspective?
>
> How did you respond?

Resilience and Lucy Hone's TED talk

Lucy Hone delivered an excellent TED talk on the subject of resilience. It's a bit odd telling someone else's story, but since she told it, and I heard it, it feels ok to pass it on.

She had studied resilience and taught it, within the US military, amongst other places. Then, after an incident involving one of her close family members, she found herself being the one needing to be resilient.

Dissatisfied with the support she was receiving from official sources she resorted to apply what she already knew, to herself.

You can watch her TED talk online to hear her in her own words but what I remember her saying was:

1. Resilient people get that s**t happens. They understand that if you are to live a life, then there will be good times and bad, easy and tough
2. Resilient people are good at making decisions in the short term that will help them get through whatever they are going through. In that respect they are kind to themselves by not making it harder than it already is
3. Resilient people are good at then focusing their attention on the things that they can influence.

These things correlate with a Harvard Business Review article I read years ago on Personal and Organisational Resilience. It said that resilience comprises three parts:

1. Facing down reality – if your situation is bad call it out as bad. Don't sugar coat it or see it through rose tinted spectacles
2. Derive learning and meaning from what you're going through and relate these to your values
3. Move forward, act, keep going, don't get stuck

It's the third one that resonated most with me – especially the not getting stuck bit, which is why Stephen Covey's Habit 1: Be Proactive, always had a lot of meaning for me.

I remember when Jim first sent me Lucy's talk. I had spent time living in a similar part of the world to where Lucy starts her story, and I can remember how it painted a vivid picture in my mind of the incident that occurred. It's a very personal, very inspiring story of a hugely difficult experience that anyone would struggle to get past.

I think we probably all want to be resilient, but it does seem to take both practice, experience, and self-awareness. I once summarised one of Jim's stories about resilience as the three A's – Accept, Adapt, and Act. That sounds quite pithy and almost easy, doesn't it?

Yet we all know that in reality, accepting a difficult situation – illness, a loss, a change in circumstances – isn't straightforward. Acceptance tends to be an ongoing cycle rather than a one-off decision, and usually something we find ourselves having to start again every time we think we have it sussed.

Adapting is also tricky – sometimes it is as simple as being kind to ourselves, and sometimes it's about having to make very difficult changes that we don't want to make. The resilience to see those changes through isn't easy but does help us get there.

Taking action to channel energy and move forward from the situation or change is really proactive, but everyone does it at their own pace. Some people will immediately put their energies into a new project after a life-changing event, and some will take their time to find the next thing to take them forward.

Resilience doesn't have a timetable, and the elements of resilience as a process aren't always linear.

When have you found yourself calling on your resilience?

How did it kick in for you?

How do you notice those around you becoming resilient?

Using your fear of failure to help you, not restrict you

I once coached a chap who was struggling to commit to some professional qualifications that he wanted to do. His company was offering to pay and to give him some time for study leave, but he was not full of confidence. He thought he could do it, but more than anything he was worried that he would not complete them - for whatever reason - and that his failure would then be quite public.

We got talking about his fear of failure.

Through our conversation, we somehow, together, came to a really helpful way of thinking for him. He began to see, and decided, that his fear of failure was really helpful to him. It helped him decide when to take risks, what to do and most of all what not to do. He also decided that he could acknowledge his fear of failure, and use it to weed out the riskiest paths, but that he could still choose to go down a path with risk if he wanted to.

On balance he decided he wanted to do the qualification, that he could do it, that he had *enough* confidence to say yes, and that he would!

The combination of self-awareness and self-acceptance gave himself the trust he needed in himself.

"If at first you don't succeed, don't take up skydiving!" was a favourite joke of mine when I first discovered it as a teenager.

There are often multiple reasons we don't or can't do things – whether through fear, lack of confidence, or even because we find them hard. Learning to look at the things that block you and find a new perspective makes it possible to learn from them, and then find that route forwards.

Like Jim's colleague, it's often more valuable to discuss these challenges with someone else who can offer some outside perspective and help us find our own route to learning from the situation. Exploring what is happening with someone who is non-judgmental is a great way to separate what is a reasonable concern from something that you could get past if you reframed the situation.

And whilst Jim's colleague took the right step forward and trusted himself, every now and then it's worth remembering that it's also OK to take a different path if you can't get past something blocking you; bungee jumping instead of skydiving!

> How have you dealt with challenges and fears that have been blockers?
>
> How did you find a new perspective?

Understanding trust by breaking it down into three parts

Sometime when my daughter was in her late teens she and her mates went for a night out in the centre of Bristol for the first time. We lived about 15-20 miles away in a small market town with just a few pubs and very little to do once they were closed.

It was a good place to grow up but as a schoolkid everyone knew everyone else's business and after a while it was very natural to want to spread your wings in the bright lights of the city.

Fortunately, my daughter had a good set of mates and though I was a little nervous I was pretty sure they would do a good job of looking out for each other and have a good time.

A couple of years later the same scenario arose with my oldest son. He also had a good set of mates, and although they were all drinkers, I figured he had a sensible head on him.

When it came to my youngest son a couple of years later still, he was younger than the other two had been at the same stage. My hesitancy must have shown because he played one of the stronger cards in his hand, "Don't you trust me?"

Trust. It's incredibly important in relationships generally and often cited for its importance in teams.

I know two very practical ways to build trust - one is to do what you say you will (and if you can't for whatever reason then explain why, as soon as you can). The other is to disclose some personal information about yourself to the other person(s) you are looking to build trust with in a relationship. I'm sure there are other ways too.

One very useful thing I once learned was called the constructs of trust. I've rarely come across it so I presume it has been more useful for me than for many others!

Instead of seeing trust as a single thing it is made up of three parts:

1. Your capacity to trust - based on your past experience (of the person or people like them)
2. Your trust in their motives - do you trust their intentions?
3. Your trust in their capability - do you trust their ability to do what they say they will?

This proved useful in my conversation with my son. By telling him I completely trusted him and his intentions made my doubts less personal. I was able to explain that my hesitancy was more about his ability to deal with situations that might arise.

In the end he went. And was fine. Turns out it was the older son I should have been more concerned about!

I was talking to friends who were all involved in a fledgling charity. They had a new volunteer on board who was incredibly enthusiastic but seemed to be trying to repeat work that had already been done instead of what was needed. This was frustrating to the existing volunteers, and damaging their trust in the new person to do what really needed to be done. Because the existing volunteers were in the majority and had done a lot of work together, they were not used to the new person not understanding where they were coming from and what had been done.

Around that time, I read a really pertinent quote; "Meet people where they are, not where you want them to be." It was really apt for the situation; the new volunteer didn't fully understand where the others had been and wanted them to understand the newbie's perspective. The experienced volunteers wanted the new person to get to where they were faster than might have been possible.

Just like Jim meeting his son where his son was and explaining the situation, the volunteers needed to be really clear about their past experiences, motives, and capabilities and vice versa in order to put everyone fully in the picture and build trust that everyone would do the right work.

How have you been able to break down a challenge to meet someone where they are? What enabled you to see the problem with that perspective?

Don't worry about things that don't need worrying about

I once knew someone, a generation older than me, who on early retirement did some part time work helping out the local undertaker, a good friend of his.

Occasionally he would be part of a conversation where someone was talking to the undertaker about their own funeral arrangements, and particularly about the cost. In some cases people were quite worried about being able to afford to have a funeral at all.

The undertaker, a very large, gregarious and caring sort, would lean forward and lower his voice, and say: "Just you remember, you don't see them lying on top".

Which is so true! It's such a great image. His words – partly in humour - were very reassuring. He was basically saying 'don't worry, we will look after you'.

You might have heard the line "I've been through some awful things in my life, some of which have actually happened", which is so true too! Spotting when our thoughts are running away with us - when we are 'catastrophising' - and changing those thoughts to more rational, more helpful ones, can be, for many, a learned skill (and often it's easier to apply when talking to someone else).

I once had a job where I worked about half an hour's drive from home, providing the traffic was ok. One morning I got to work and was convinced I'd left my hair straighteners switched on because I couldn't remember switching them off. I called my boss and told him I'd have to go home because my flat was probably already on fire. I jumped in the car and promptly got caught in traffic, convinced that due to the delays the whole block of flats would be on fire and my neighbours would be furious. When I eventually arrived home there was no sign of any fire engines and nothing was on fire. The hair straighteners were not even switched on; either I had turned them off automatically or they had a shut-down function.

My brain had completely made up a scenario and tortured me with it because I was on autopilot.

Compare that to a Friday afternoon a year or so later, and having left the office a little early, I walked into my flat to find it slightly smoky. I'd prepared breakfast and lunch on the hob that morning, put the pan back on a low heat full of water just to loosen off any debris, and promptly forgotten about it. It was lucky that although it had been burning all day and the water was long gone, it hadn't actually combusted by the time I got home! I had absolutely no idea that I'd forgotten to turn the stove off.

I've learned from this to try and be more conscious when I am doing things before leaving the house – making a mental note of locking the door for example, to help me stop catastrophising about what I might have forgotten to do. And I've also been able to use the example of the pan being on the stove all day and still not setting the place on fire, to remind me that the worst doesn't always happen.

How have you catastrophised in the past?

What helped you learn to spot those thoughts and how did you learn to mitigate them?

4 CHOICES

"Now and then it's good to pause in our pursuit of happiness and just be happy."

GUILLAUME APOLLINAIRE

"It is our choices Harry, that show what we truly are, far more than our abilities."

DUMBLEDORE

"You can't leap a chasm in two jumps"

ANON

"Life rewards action, not intelligence. Many brilliant people talk themselves out of getting started, and being smart doesn't help very much without the courage to act. You can't win if you're not in the game."

JAMES CLEAR

All the stories in this section relate in some way to choices - having choices, recognising choices and making choices.

Choices are a key factor in our performance at work and in our lives.

I've come to believe that there are always choices, even if some are difficult or unpalatable. So stories to illustrate the choices we make can help in both broadening perspective and making decisions.

Choices when making critical decisions

Back in the mid 90s I knew a chap in his very early 30s who was already a qualified Consultant Paediatrician working at a large hospital in the north of England.

At the time I was working in financial services. I reckon I could have made the "wrong decision" all day every day for a week and the consequences would have been minimal. Certainly not catastrophic for me or anyone else.

About that time I asked the Consultant about the decisions he had to make every day in a hospital, full of pretty sick children. I was curious about how he coped with what felt like to me must be enormous pressure. I clearly remember the two parts of his answer:

1. The training he'd had. He said this meant he was pretty ready to make decisions and had enough confidence to do so
2. At the point a decision needed making a decision needed making. He said if someone was there who was better qualified or more experienced to make the decision, then they would make the decision. But failing that he would.

It struck me then that he was pretty clear in his thinking. It strikes me now that it was a great two part combination for coping with the life and death decisions he was making on a daily basis.

Clear strategies for coping with pressure can be learned, trained or stumbled upon. However they've originated, they're very helpful!

When you've had formal training like a doctor or nurse will have had, it seems as if you would have a clear idea about whether you knew what you were doing or not. For many people however, their careers evolve over time and we gradually accumulate much of the knowledge and experience we need to become experts. This can lead to a lack of confidence in your own abilities and expertise – perhaps because you haven't had it formally bestowed upon you, or the lack of certification and formality that you might get at school, university, or on a training course.

Often, when people who are very experienced in a specific career get asked how they made a certain decision, they'll say "Well, it's just common sense, isn't it?" I've heard common sense referred to as 'years of experience, compressed' – and this type of expertise is sometimes called tacit or implicit knowledge; things we know because of the experiences we've had.

Sometimes the very nature of tacit knowledge and the informal nature of acquiring it can make us second guess our authority when it comes to taking critical decisions. It can be hard to know whether we are indeed the most qualified person around to make that tough call.

> How often do you take a step back and think about the choices you have available to you? How often do you ask yourself if you're the right person to make a decision, even when you know what the answer must be?
>
> What would give you confidence that you are the right person to make the call?
>
> How would you know what a more experienced person looks like?

There are always choices even if one or more is pretty unappealing

I've come to learn that there are always choices. Even when it feels you have none, there is always an alternative - no matter how dire and no matter how bad the consequences. I find that recognising the choice is usually helpful.

By way of example, when my daughter turned 16, my youngest son then aged 11, asked if that meant she could leave home. Quite a grown up and inquisitive question I thought.

"Yes", I told him, "she could leave home". He was silent, thinking.

"Then again", I went on, "you could leave home anytime too. The door is not bolted, you could just open it and go".

There was another silence. I could see the wheels turning in his head.

"Mind you", I continued, "you would have to find a place to sleep, and your food to eat".

He stayed.

But there are always choices. I think this is always true, and often worth reminding yourself of.

One of my favourite stories from the Buddhist traditions is as follows: Two monks, one older and very experienced, and one younger and very fervent, were walking to another monastery. They came to a river where an old woman was struggling to cross the high water. The monks were forbidden to have anything to do with women, let alone touch them. The younger monk prepared to cross, leaving her struggling. Then the older monk, to the younger monk's horror, carried the woman across the river. He placed her down safely, waited for the younger monk to cross, and they resumed their journey. The younger monk fumed as they walked — "Why did he break his vows? Why isn't he explaining himself? How will the abbot respond when he finds out? Will I be in trouble too? Why didn't he just leave her there, someone else would have helped?"

Eventually, the younger monk couldn't contain his anger, and turning to the older monk, asked "Why on earth did you break your vow and touch that woman back at the river?" The older monk simply said, "My brother, I put the woman down once we had crossed the river. You have carried her all the way here."

We always have choices, both practically and in how we respond to any given situation. They might not be easy choices, and they might not be attractive choices, but they are within your power.

> How do you explore your choices when things seem tough?
> What influences you?

Alternative, unanticipated choices are sometimes available if you look or listen

There are always choices. I once caught a train from Bristol Parkway to London Paddington. It was a journey I would do every few weeks. Sometimes the train was on time and often a few minutes late. Occasionally very late.

On this occasion, as we came to a stop, the train conductor made an announcement to all the passengers:

"Ladies and gentlemen, I'm pleased to tell you that we have arrived at our destination four minutes early. But if you are feeling short-changed, you are welcome to stay on the train".

I liked that. I chose to get off along with everyone else ☺ but we always have choices!

Working within any business or formal organisation that employs tens or hundreds of people is fascinating. Whilst every organisation and its culture are different, it's always fascinating to identify the strengths and weaknesses of the way things are done. I've worked in organisations that it seemed had lost sight of their core purpose; but no-one held them to account for that and it didn't seem to be a problem. I've worked in organisations where the level of trust in each employee to be at their best was incredibly high, and organisations where it wasn't.

One organisation I have worked at was fascinating because it was full of deeply expert, passionate people. Collectively, they all wanted to do their best, and to solve every problem or take every opportunity that crossed their desk. That made it a very inspiring place to work, but at the same time, very poor at acknowledging success or good work. It wasn't that no-one wanted to acknowledge it, but that they were so entirely focused on either refining the outcome further in order to perfect it, or on the next project or problem they needed to move on to. It made it very hard to stop, reflect, and give each other – and themselves- the praise that was deserved for their hard work.

Whether unexpected – like the train conductor announcing the train was early – or just an expected outcome that you've worked hard for, it can be so easy to just move on to the next thing.

How often do you stop and reflect on successes?

Who do you share the success with?

Take care making a choice for short term gain if there is a longer term loss

We're having to make choices all the time.

When it comes to our physical health, and in particular, what we eat, I clearly remember an ex-colleague saying that "the world is working against us". He was pointing out that we're constantly being marketed unhealthy foods, containing fats and sugars, and often both, and more than we need.

So to eat well we have to make conscious choices, because if we don't, the world will encourage us to eat too much stuff that's not good for us.

The same is true of activity and exercise. There are more and more labour-saving devices which mean that if we wanted to lead a very sedentary lifestyle we can. In my lifetime I can think of TV remote controls, travelators at airports, power drills, dishwashers, bikes with motors…

And the same is even true of sleep. Once upon a time TV used to finish at midnight, or around then, and there was no internet. Now the world is 24 hours. When I was young if we thought about phoning someone in the evening, but it was past 9.00pm, we would say that it was too late and call the next day. Now we're sending, and picking up, messages at all hours.

And sometimes in our busyness we can make odd choices about what to eat and drink. We can be so busy that we make poor choices in both the short and longer term.

Once in talking to a group of people at a customer business, we got onto the subject of nutrition and hydration and how, if we want to perform at our best – to be able to concentrate well and to make good decisions – we need to keep our blood sugar levels at a reasonable level and make sure we drink enough.

Two ladies, in customer facing roles, explained that they were so busy, that they couldn't afford to be away from their desks. To help them they had stopped drinking anything, all day, so that they didn't have to go to the loo.

I suggested that they had a word with themselves.

Not drinking was giving them more time at their desk but probably at the expense of concentration and other negative side effects. I can't remember what they did as a result of the conversation, but it highlighted the habit they had slipped into.

Unhealthy habits we have slipped into – especially regarding what we eat and drink – can be performance killers. And making short term decisions – or not! - can have long term negative impact.

(As I heard Tony Blackburn say: "I crossed a crocodile with a homing pigeon and I'm afraid it's going to come back and bite me.)

It's been fascinating to watch discussions about the pros and cons of working from home over the last few years. Up until shortly before the pandemic hit, I felt strongly that I didn't want to work from home. I enjoyed being around others in the office and felt I would be too isolated at home and find it hard to focus.

I was surprised to find that I could work effectively from home, but it took me a long time to accept that stepping away from my computer to wander into the garden in summer, or to transfer a load of washing, or nip down to the local pharmacy for a prescription wasn't 'cheating' my employer of my time. I actually needed the short time away from my screen to clear my head, process my thoughts, and have a screen break. I started reading at lunchtime, even if only for 5 minutes, because it felt beneficial to use my imagination and immerse myself into a different world and completely forget about work for a few moments.

Whether it's drinking enough, giving your eyes and your mind a break, or eating well, sometimes it can be really hard to get your personal recipe for success at work spot on. External and internal influences can push us towards the wrong choices, and it can be hard to change habits when you feel as if it would be 'wrong' to try something different.

> What is your personal recipe for achieving your best performance at work?
>
> What do you need to eat and drink, and how often do you need to take breaks?
>
> Do you need to talk to someone else to get into 'work mode' or do you prefer to have undisturbed silence to get things done?

When to change course – luck and judgement in making decisions

I enjoyed Charles Handy's story of Davy's Bar as told towards the start of his book, The Second Curve. The book is about when an organisation (or product, or whatever), that is on an upward curve, needs to do something different *before* the curve starts to flatten, in order to experience a second upward curve.

In the story the author is driving on a small road in southern Ireland and stops to ask a local chap for directions. The chap says it's along here, past that turn, down that hill etc. He then explains that the author will pass Davy's Bar, but half a mile before that, he has to turn right. The author winds up the window and continues before realising the flaw in the directions.

Often the path is not clear and we just have to make a choice, based on our best guess, and hope.

Sometimes a decision is needed. Sometimes we can apply the oblique strategy "do nothing for as long as possible" but that's still a strategy (as opposed to doing something). But sometimes we just need to decide and be done with it.

A friend of mine once had a major dilemma regarding a family business he was a part of. As he wrestled with what to do I tried to offer him the comfort that whatever happened, I would remind him in the future about how big a dilemma it was, and how the best path to follow was far from obvious.

Years later he offered me the same advice when my path was very clearer.

I often talk to leaders about their careers, the decisions they've made, and the paths they've followed. We frequently comment that these paths that lead us to a particular position or role only ever make sense in hindsight; that you take a choice in your life because it seems to be the best option on the table. Most senior leaders don't start their career planning to be the CFO or COO of a 400-person company by the time they are aged X. Only when they reflect on their whole career path is it easy to draw connections or identify that a skill or opportunity in one place was valuable years down the line.

It can be easy to struggle with a difficult decision because you don't have any idea of what the future will hold. It can be hard to justify a decision that seems to be going badly with the reasoning that it will make much more sense as part of a longer timeline in future. Sometimes the best thing you can do is to talk it over with someone else acting as a sounding board – especially if they are willing to discuss it with you in the future, as Jim offered to do for his friend. Having someone to explore your justifications with can be much more helpful than someone telling you what the right or wrong answer is – although the latter can be useful to provoke a visceral response and identify your gut instincts!

When did you last ask someone to be a sounding board for a tough decision, and how did that help you?

And when did you last act as a sounding board for someone else?

Choosing a one-off behavioural strategy for a very specific occasion

Sometimes we make tactical decisions about our behaviour. We calculate what strategy will give us the best chance to achieve our goal. And sometimes the path we choose is out of our comfort zone but we do it anyway.

Back in about 2002 the football team I supported as a boy and into adulthood, Southampton, reached the English FA Cup Final. I had managed to go to the semi-final, with a long-time friend, Ric, who knew someone – who knew someone - who worked for the FA, who had got us a pair of tickets.

Getting tickets for semi-finals and finals can be about who you know.

My long-time friend Ric had managed to get a ticket for the final but not one for me this time. I had pretty much ruled out getting to the game as it felt like my options were pretty limited. However I knew that the large corporate business I worked for, AXA, had two debenture tickets at the ground where they were playing the final (that year it was the Millennium stadium in Cardiff while Wembley was being renovated) and that whoever would be using them was at the discretion of the alpha male sales director.

So the day after the semi-final I made a plan to ask him for the tickets. Although he could be totally charming he was also a no nonsense guy. So I approached his office with a lot of nerves, trepidation (being the more introverted, not so assertive, sort) but also very focused.

I knocked on the open door and he looked up from his desk.

"What do you want?" he asked, quite abruptly.

I had anticipated his directness and knew that I needed to be direct back. But I was ready.

"I want your FA Cup Final tickets", I replied (telling myself to shut up and not say anything else). His demeanour actually softened a fraction.

"Who would you take?" he asked, again.

Bugger, I thought, I hadn't planned this far!

"Not sure". I feebly replied, my position very much weakened.

But I'd done enough, for now, because he told me to "go away and think about it". An olive branch.

It was a 10 second conversation. I was closer and had not blown it, yet!

I saw him the next day, this time on an escalator, and was ready again for another short conversation.

"I know who I will take", I offered.

"Who's that?" he said.

"Anyone you want me to" I said.

"Good answer", he replied with a smile.

"Go away and find a big customer to take, who supports your team, and the tickets are yours".

And so I did. The final wasn't a great game, and my team lost, but I was grateful to be there.

The one off strategy for the very specific scenario had worked very well on that occasion.

I was speaking to a very senior leader recently – the kind of person who is in such a senior position in the sector that they are likely to be recognised in the street by strangers. We spoke about what it was like to be at the top, and in particular, how to approach key figures in government who have said quite unpleasant things about your sector. I asked how on earth it would be possible to go into a meeting with senior government figures after some of these pronouncements and have a productive meeting.

The answer that came back was "Kill them with kindness. Don't let on for a second that their rhetoric has affected you. Make your points robustly, but treat your counterparts as fellow humans, and leave them where you found them." And as one of those senior ministers had been shuffled out of cabinet, they had apparently turned to my interviewee and said "We may have agreed to disagree, but we always did it as friends."

I'm not sure I could quite manage that – I've hardly got a poker face! But taking on a challenging situation when you know how you are going to play it makes it a very different ball game. Not only were my interviewee's tactics robust, but they were both proactive and had an element of defence built in. This person knew exactly how they were going into the encounter, and what they wanted from it, as well as how they had to achieve it.

How often do you have to deal with challenges like this?

Do you plan how you're going to act and respond, or do you expect that you'll be able to react appropriately in the moment?

Have you ever come out of a situation wishing you'd considered your strategy ahead of time?

Choosing where to go to do your best work

I heard Rebecca Romero presenting at a work event once. She was the guest speaker, and was an international athlete. Unusually she had competed for GB as a rower, winning a silver medal at the Athens Olympics, before switching to track cycling, where she won a gold in Beijing.

I don't know the full story but from what I understand she was unhappy in the rowing set up. Although she won an Olympic medal something wasn't quite right for her. I imagine it was a big decision for her to switch sports.

The line she used, which I remember, was "instead of trying to blossom where you are planted, plant yourself where you can blossom".

Such a simple and powerful idea, which the phrase captures so well.

My coaching and consulting work has taken me into a multitude of different organisations, sectors and industries. They are all different. (So much so that each one says they are unique!)

Sometimes there are people in organisations and cultures that seem just made for them. Happy days. But I've seen other people like fish out of water, sometimes at a cost to their health. On my first teaching practice during my PGCE year I came across some long standing teachers who were surviving but clearly not enjoying their work and who had lost their appetite for education in the state schools of that time.

After 15 years working in financial services, the many subsequent years has shown me that it's a big wide world out there. If you are unhappy, stressed or unfulfilled it might well be at least worth keeping open to new possibilities. Like Rebecca Romero.

Several years ago I was considering the next step in my career. I was in a role that I felt I'd mastered, had taken plenty of learning and growth opportunities that had come my way, and didn't feel I could grow much more – or blossom – by staying where I was. I looked around at what I could do, but struggled to find a direction to move into. I thought about an MBA, but with several degrees under my belt already, I didn't feel I could justify the cost or time out. A friend of mine recommended a career coach she knew, and as the coach was still qualifying, she offered me some free sessions.

It was a really valuable process to go through – we both enjoyed the experience – and we tried to look at multiple options for the types of work that I liked and was good at. As part of this process, the coach asked me to close my eyes and visualise what my ideal surroundings and work would be like. I found that really useful – because although I didn't know what type of work I'd be doing, I visualised a sunny room and a team I was part of, working together on something exciting. It will be no surprise to you that my office at that time was in a basement with no windows!

As it happened, I didn't leave that organisation for a while – an opportunity came up and I happily spent another couple of years there. But thinking about the type of place I wanted to plant myself in order to blossom was very valuable.

What conditions would you need to plant yourself in so that you could blossom?

Eating well – keeping it simple and obvious

A few years ago, in the car, on the way home from Bristol Parkway train station after a day working in London, I heard a guy on the radio talking about food. I was interested in the subject. I was (and am) aware that many of us in the west don't eat particularly healthily, or as healthily as we could. The speaker was a nutritionist, and American, and I think he was plugging a book, so my scepticism radar was switched to high.

I remember he said he had some 'rules', or guidelines, for eating, that I thought were really good.

About 10 years later, in 2020, I was watching University Challenge on TV over the Christmas period, with university alumni teams taking part. One of the questions was, "Complete the last three words of this seven-word sentence: "Eat food, mainly plants,..."

The answer was "not too much."

A couple of days later I was mentioning this question to my friend Nick, who lives in Cincinnati, who is married to a nutritionist (and an American), and he immediately said "that's Michael Pollan". So I looked up Michael Pollan and sure enough he was the same guy I remembered from the radio all those years before, because some of the rules were on his website.

The ones I remember from the radio interview are:

- Always sit down to eat when you can
- Always eat with others when you can
- Spend more eat less (so spend your money on good quality food when you can, rather than junk food)
- Don't buy food with more than five ingredients (try and buy the constituent parts and put your food together – rather than buy processed foods)
- Beware all food claiming health benefits
- Don't eat anything your great, great, great grandmother wouldn't recognise as food

On the back of hearing the interview in the car, I noticed in our local Tesco supermarket a couple of adjacent signs hanging from the ceiling in one of the aisles. One sign said 'Cereals' and the other, further down, said 'Healthy Cereals'. In this case the 'Cereals' were all the sugar coated, highly processed, salted ones and the 'Healthy Cereals" were the granola, bran and muesli etc.

I wanted to get a big, thick, black pen and write the word 'Unhealthy' on the 'Cereals' sign.

Finally, I remember Mark, a third-year student in my flat in my first year, and a good cook, who says he was taught to ask "Where's the colour?" (on the plate) as a way of seeking to ensure there was enough nutrition. Beige and brown for energy (potatoes, pasta, rice) and colour for nutrition.

Eating well is not always easy given the environment, who we live with, our budget and other factors. But Michael Pollan's 'rules' are helpful.

Since writing the above I have read Michael Pollan's *Food Rules* (2009). It's a short, simple and powerful read. The most impactful book I've read in a while.

In my dim and distant past, I was a rugby player in a mid-tier team for several years. It was a great group; serious about doing our best on the pitch but friendly and welcoming off the pitch. A lot of that culture was down to our captain, Maria. She ruled the team with an iron fist, but was also the first in line for fun and games. She sadly died a few years ago of a brain haemorrhage whilst cycling home from work, having taken up the saddle after rugby.

Every year, the rugby team would go on tour together over the May bank holiday weekend. My first tour with this team was to Viadana, a small village in Lombardy in Italy. Being a fairly small locale, we were unusually dependent on being bussed around to various activities and locations that had been arranged for us, rather than on other tours to cities where there would be more free time and choice of activities. This meant that our meals were in some interesting places – a pizza and wine bar (that decided to stay open as long as the team were drinking there the night before the tour match), a rugby club, an agriturismo that produced its own charcuterie, vinegar and oils, and so on. What proved increasingly difficult was being served anything green or leafy – Maria very pointedly complained that the food was "all beige." Of course this led to many future "beige food" pranks and jokes, but it was a serious point that would ring in my ears every year as I got home from tour and headed to the shops to fill the fridge from the fruit and veg section.

Situations like rugby tours or holidays are often an exception to our normal healthy eating choices, and there's nothing wrong with that. What I've found important is to note how eating unhealthy food for a few days makes me feel, and to think about ways I can counter that. Sometimes it's easier to make a good choice – when I last visited the USA, I ate out a fair bit during part of my trip to a National Park as it was hard to shop and store food, but by choosing to order salads I realised that I was feeling much less sluggish than if I just chose the easiest option.

> How do food choices affect you, and how do you find a balance when healthy options aren't easy?

Strategy and risk – an example from *Will It Make the Boat Go Faster?*

The best book I've ever read on team performance is Will It Make The Boat Go Faster? by Ben Hunt-Davis and Hilary Beveridge. Their Olympic experience is full of great stories, including one about how a failing strategy (just train harder) wasn't moving them closer to their goal (win Olympic gold) so they were forced to innovate and change (one of the textbook benefits of goals).

I like the story of how they changed their thinking, to make it more helpful, so that whatever happened, including things going awry, they were able say "that's good because...". E.g. we lost that race. That's good because, we've learned xyz...

But in particular I like the story of their tactics going into the final – "the biggest race of their lives". Choosing their tactics for such an important race was a big decision that required clarity and complete unity.

I don't want to tell the story here in full, suffice to say that the tactics they chose, and put into place, were only possible because of their assessment of risk, their desire to win, and all the preparation and teamwork which meant that there was complete trust within the eight-man crew.

The whole book is a great story, and well worth a read if you and/or your team want to get better.

If you have read and liked Will It Make The Boat Go Faster? You might also like The Boys In The Boat. Not a business book, but also a true story and a great historical work.

I met my close friend Liz when we were three years old, at nursery school. We went to the same small primary school, and then to the same secondary school in the next town. We lived a few minutes' walk from each other in the same small town until I was about 13, and as we got to the end of primary school, would often spend the day together at the weekend. When our parents thought we were old enough, we would walk a mile to the local swimming pool on a Saturday, spend the afternoon swimming, and then walk home via the local 'Tuck Shop', picking up some penny sweets to eat at her house in front of Saturday early evening 90's classics like Baywatch – TV that I definitely wasn't allowed to watch at home! Often her parents would invite me to stay for dinner too – a real treat.

At high school, we had a gym class that involved working in pairs on a routine – each pair would have to move into various positions and lift and balance each other to show strength and agility. The teacher decided to film us doing these routines, and then talked the class through each one to explain how she was marking them and what she was looking for us to achieve.

As each video was played, the teacher would point out every time that a pair would interrupt their focus to check where their partner was and whether they were doing the right thing at the right time. Liz and I performed our routine together and as our video was played through, the teacher pointed out various mistakes, technical errors and things that went slightly wrong. At the end, she asked the class if they'd noticed that not once had she called their attention to us breaking focus or looking for each other during the routine. We had trusted each other completely.

That might not seem like a huge achievement, but it's one that I remain proud of several decades later. We're still friends, by the way!

> Have you ever been in a team with complete trust?
>
> How did that feel, and what did that trust enable you to achieve?

Getting the input of others in your decisions

Get lots of advice but remember you don't have to follow it. I think on balance, making decisions about your own life and future is more empowering and ultimately more satisfying. Of course you can choose to follow advice, but it's still you that is choosing.

I once watched a fascinating programme on Channel 4, which I think was one of a short series of three or four, though I only caught the one episode.

It focused on a dairy farmer, in his 30s. He was single-handedly running the farm on behalf of his two very elderly uncles. His uncles lived on the farm and he lived with his girlfriend nearby. Being a dairy farmer he worked very long hours, and all hours, including a *very* early start.

His dilemma was whether to stay or go. His heart told him he needed to continue. Loyalty, inertia and other forces were compelling him to stay. But his head, and his girlfriend were telling him something else. His very understanding girlfriend felt he was being paid a pittance and taken for granted.

And the premise of the programme? Bizarrely, 100 ordinary people followed him round – literally, for a few days. They observed him, listened to him, chatted to him, and were part of the discussions about his future that he was having with his uncles and with his girlfriend. They went through the mud with him and crammed into his house and the farmhouse to eavesdrop.

At the end, they told him totally openly, honestly and objectively what they thought he should do. Pretty much unanimously they felt he should go.

This way of helping to decide something feels useful. You might argue it's a cop out, but it was still the farmer, in the end, deciding. The combination of understanding, total honesty and unbiased advice is rare. If we are lucky we can get it – from friends, family and colleagues. But that is to be fortunate indeed.

The farmer left.

Sometimes the input of others is invaluable in ways that they – and you - can't imagine! I bought a new car a few months ago, and as I don't drive much at the moment, it was a tricky decision to make. I weighed up the pros and cons, and apart from being able to get a decent return for selling my old (but Ultra Low Emission Zone compliant) car, it didn't make that much practical sense.

My family all advised me not to do it, and in doing so, cemented my decision to go for it. I knew not buying the car would disappoint me after spending so long researching it, especially as I was finding my old car increasingly tricky to drive. Changing to a more comfortable automatic with cruise control made driving a lot easier for me, and it was a choice I could afford to make. I haven't regretted it for a moment, and whilst I appreciate my family's generosity of time and consideration in advising me, it only served to help me be certain of the choice I made.

> When has listening to the advice of others allowed you to make the opposite decision?
>
> Was it the right one?

Being careful what you say out loud as a leader / manager / coach or parent

The coach's words – or the words of anyone who is influential in someone else's life, like a manager or leader – can be very powerful. As one ex-colleague pointed out to me, the coach's words can become the performer's self-talk.

This puts the coach in a position of great responsibility. Taking care with any feedback or advice - positioning it, checking how it has been received, delivering it with care - is a key consideration and challenge.

I think this can be particularly true when the coachee is either young, or impressionable, or lacking confidence or struggling with something (where they can be looking for answers or quick fixes).

I was at a coaching conference once where two speakers each told a powerful story from their own personal experience.

First up was former Olympic gold medal winning swimmer Adrian Moorhouse. He talked about going to his local swimming pool/club as a young boy, when he was far from being even the best swimmer in his age group. One day he was asked by one of the swimming coaches why he came to swimming club. "Because I want to swim at the Olympics and win a gold medal", was his reply.

He said two important things happened next.

Firstly, the coach didn't laugh at him. He said the coach respected his goal and took his ambitions seriously.

The second was that the coach said to him: "Well in that case you are going to have to work really, really hard."

The second speaker I remember had a job title of something like Director of Coaching at PWC or another such big organisation.

In his story he explained how he had been a very good youth rugby player. He represented Wales at Under 18 level (in the back row, as an open side flanker). Then one day the coaches spoke to him about their concerns over his size. At that time the top players in his position were getting bigger and, in particular, taller. They had looked at his parents, and in particular the height of his mother – apparently a greater indicator of ultimate height – and advised him to change position, to prop, which he agreed to do.

As things turned out, he never went on to play for the full Welsh international team.

Years later he said he was at a motorway service station, taking a pee, when he looked to the right at the man standing there next to him. He immediately recognised him as Neil Back, the highly successful English and British Lions rugby player, *who played in his original position*, before his coaches advised him to move.

And he was a couple of inches taller than Neil Back.

He told the story not with any hint of blame towards the coaches, but simply to illustrate the impact that the coach can have.

I have my own example, of Mrs Brown at primary school. During rehearsals for a school Christmas play she said there was a problem and told me, and two others to stop. When everyone sang without the three of us she said it was much better. I thought this might at least mean we were excused rehearsals but she said we had to learn the words and mime.

I'm not sure how she might have handled it differently, but hers was a different approach to the swimming club coach.

As coaches, leaders, managers or parents, we can, if we choose, be free with our suggestions and advice but, if we are, we need to take a reasonable amount of responsibility for its impact. Words delivered without thought, or in frustration or naivety, can have lasting and potentially damaging impact.

I was once chatting to an old schoolfriend who I hadn't spoken to in several years. We talked about hopes and aspirations, and it became clear that she was going to tell me about a hobby that she was passionate about, because she told me not to laugh when she told me about it. When she did tell me about this hobby, I was perplexed because I couldn't see anything funny about someone enjoying a craft and acquiring expertise in it. I encouraged her interest and let her know that I was impressed by her expertise.

We were talking again a few months later, and I mentioned that I had just spotted a new camera lens on offer and was thinking of buying it. The response was a scathing "Well, you're hardly David Bailey, are you?"

On reflection, maybe my former friend was just echoing the responses she was used to hearing from the people around her – especially as she had expected me to respond derisively to her hobby. As I'd never wanted to be a portrait photographer let alone a professional one, there were aspects of the response I could ignore – after all, I was taking photographs for my own enjoyment and it was a bonus if others liked them too. But as a comment from someone I trusted and respected at that time, my confidence in my photography skills took a real blow for a while.

These comments often slip out unguarded, as Jim says, in the heat of the moment or whilst preoccupied elsewhere. But the damage they can do is immense, especially if the recipient is young. Of course we're all human, and we all make mistakes. Often a sincere apology can repair the damage if we find out we've made a mistake – and the repair can lead to greater trust in the long term.

> Have you ever found yourself saying something you wish you hadn't?
>
> How did you repair those words?

People can be unpredictable in their behaviour – but can you still choose your response?

There are many things out of your control - including other people - their perspectives, personalities, biases, thinking, values and their responses. What you can try and do is control your responses to other people's seemingly irrational, unreasonable or even bizarre behaviour.

This can be challenging and is often easier said than done.

A few years ago I was part of a team running a conference for a large group of about 500 people. My two colleagues had worked closely with the leadership team to plan and deliver the day. All was going well until one of the leadership team reported to us that there had been a complaint, from one of the delegates, that the presentations, and the day, had had an overly male bias.

We were flabbergasted and my male colleague, who was hosting the sessions on the main stage and had delivered a presentation of his own, was stunned and not a little insulted. The fact that he/we had arranged for Katherine Grainger to be the main speaker seemed lost on the delegate.

The feedback threatened to have a very negative impact on my colleague, on us and on the day. It felt completely unjust.

However the male colleague was then very well supported in the moment by our female colleague, and also the female HR Director, who both reassured him that the content was fine, that they were happy and that, crucially, it was difficult to account for the isolated views of one person. My female colleague pointed out that if someone is sitting with a fixed agenda, to look out for and find bias, then they are likely, at least in their own mind, to find it.

The support to the colleague in the moment was very helpful, and though still taken aback, and a little put out, he was able to compose himself and see the comment for what it was. At that point he was back in control again and focused.

It would have been very difficult for him to do this on his own, but getting the input and perspective of others really helped.

The complaint had seemed weird and out of context but was difficult to ignore. *Collectively* we chose our response pretty well.

Way back a decade or two ago, I was playing a mid-level rugby match. As a front-row forward, most of my work in the game was at breakdowns and the set-piece, helping protect the ball so that the backs could use it most effectively.

On this day, I had been in a ruck, and as the ball moved away the players on the floor started to get up. As I started to run off to follow the ball, I realised that one of the opposition players was holding my arm tightly with her hand and seemed reluctant to let go. As I started to move towards the current play, she followed me, still holding on.

I looked quizzically at her, and asked her to let go.

No dice.

After a while, I used the flat underside of my other forearm to push against her arm, saying loudly 'Let go'.

This didn't work, so I pulled my arm away and then repeated the action and the words.

To my surprise, this girl turned her head and shouted to the passing referee, "Ref, she's hitting me!"

The referee looked over, apprised the situation, and simply said "Well… Let go then."

She did.

Bizarre story, right? It was a situation I only encountered once in about ten years of playing rugby, and it clearly was just as nonsensical to the referee as it was to me. The player in question clearly just had a bit of a moment of madness, and probably didn't set out to do something so pointless. Yet it had happened – and the referee's response confirmed that it was unnecessary behaviour that didn't need to happen. If the referee had turned around and sent me off for hitting the other player, I suppose it would have been memorable for very different reasons!

Who do you look to for perspective when someone around you acts in an unexpected way?

How does that response help you adapt to the situation?

5 MOTIVATION

'If I kick my dog [from the front or the back], he will move. And when I want him to move again, what must I do? I must kick him again. Similarly, I can charge a man's battery, and then recharge it, and recharge it again. But it is only when he has his own generator that we can talk about motivation. He then needs no outside stimulation. He wants to do it".

Herzberg

Like confidence, motivation can be a slippery beast. I know this well as someone who at one point was completing a master's dissertation on the subject and had just about given up!

Motivation at work and in life is clearly a critical factor in what you do, for how long and how well. Some understanding of it seems incredibly helpful.

I like the stories in this section because they all have a practical element, linking a massive, broad subject to real situations.

Whose job is it to motivate who??

A few years ago I worked with a senior leadership team in one part of a very large UK business. I spent a couple of days with them talking about high performing teams and at one point on day one, when discussing motivation, I asked them "do you need your boss to motivate you?" They all said 'no'. After all, these were leaders I was talking to.

On day two we were talking about their leadership role – what it was and what it wasn't. I asked them if it was their job to motivate their teams, and they all said 'yes'.

A couple of weeks later I was working with the Ops Director from that leadership team and all the Regional Managers that reported to him. I asked them the same questions in the same order. On day 1, "Do you need your boss to motivate you?", "No". On day 2, "Is it your job to motivate your teams?", "Yes".

And a couple of weeks later I was working with the District Managers who reported to the Regional Managers. I asked them "Do you need your boss to motivate you?", and they said "No". And later I asked them "Is it your job to motivate your teams?", and they said "Yes".

Shortly after that I got to start working with the Team Leaders who reported to the District Managers and I got the same responses to my questions. It seemed like no-one felt like they needed their boss to motivate them but that everyone felt it was their job to motivate to their teams!

It led to some really useful questions:
- What would happen if you stopped trying to motivate your teams? and
- What do you need from your boss?

The second question led to some valuable answers. People felt they needed various things from their boss at different times. Sometimes a sense of direction – "where is the company heading, and where are we heading, as far as you know?". Sometimes they need help – "can you ask so-and-so to provide this information or explain why it's important we get it quickly?". Sometimes they need training or coaching – "how do I...?". And sometimes they need support or encouragement – "I'm stuck with... or I don't feel confident with...".

There are other things of course. But leaders and team leaders who provide these things – helping people have purpose, feel empowered and feel capable – are being very motivational, without actually making it their job to motivate.

What do you need from your boss? And how has that changed over the years?

Like everyone, I've had an interesting range of bosses. I suspect one of my first bosses stood up for me in the face of a senior leader who wanted to bully me, and because of that ended up suddenly leaving a job they were very good at after many years, rather than participate in the bully's plan.

Another boss generally left me to my own devices, but one day managed to time a visit to my office absolutely perfectly – I was dealing with a difficult caller late on a Friday afternoon and this caller was so exasperated by my not being able to do what he asked (I think he wanted someone to agree that his council were racist for demanding he pay council tax…), that he demanded to speak to my boss. I was sure my boss would have gone home for the weekend, but at that moment he suddenly walked into my office.

I held out the phone and said: "This person would like to speak to you…." My boss listened to the caller, told him that he was wrong and that it didn't matter who he spoke to as he wasn't going to like the answer, and ended the call. I couldn't have asked for anything more at that moment!

These examples have helped me shape my own style as a manager, and I've always felt it is critical for my team to know I have their back and will support them if they need to escalate something or ask for help. And from the feedback I've had, they appreciate it.

What have your leaders and managers done for you that is memorable?

How has that shaped you as a performer, and if you are one, as a manager?

Coaches can only really help if you are motivated

I have occasionally had alarm bells ringing when a leader has asked me to coach one of their team to get the team member to do something. In this scenario the manager has been ineffective in enabling behaviour change – for whatever reason – and has turned to an external coach instead.

In these circumstances it's not the coach's job to replace the leader or manager and to try and convince the team member, or "coach them", to change.

In these circumstances the only joke I know about coaching rings true. It goes like this:

"How many coaches does it take to change a lightbulb?"

"Only one, but the lightbulb has to really want to change"

It's difficult, if not impossible, to coach someone who doesn't want to be coached or who refuses to change. If you're a coach then that's worth knowing, so you can decide what you want to do (and not take it personally if you don't see results).

Back in my rugby playing days, I remember getting briefly frustrated with our coaches one evening. They were absolutely brilliant and dedicated volunteers who not only gave up their free time to coach us, but were also committed to learning and growing in their coaching practice. They were very focused on being effective rather than necessarily sticking to the tried and tested, and it was usually incredibly refreshing. They were also very successful, had taken the team to new heights, and had high standards.

One of my favourite things about these coaches was that they had realised that playing any kind of game as a warm-up was far more effective and motivating than sending us to run laps. As someone who hated running, it was far easier to push myself playing 'rugby netball', touch rugby, or tag, and therefore get warmed up effectively. They also had a great initiative called 'the cynical post' whereby anyone cheating in training would have to run to the far side of the training ground and round a lamppost – an incredibly effective deterrent penalty!

On this occasion, I was frustrated because we were learning a new move in training. We started running through it in small groups, and the first time I tried it, I got it wrong. I'm pretty sure I got it wrong the second time as well. The coaches called out to me to remind me what to do. I was frustrated because I knew what to do in theory and wanted to get it right, but it also felt like it was going to take me several practice runs to master it. I just needed to be left to keep practicing in order to master it in my own time, rather than in two attempts.

After sharing this feedback with the coaches via the captain, they – to their credit – started to give me a bit more time to get used to new skills. I wasn't necessarily easy to coach (or maybe not as easy as the rest of the team!) but seeing that I wanted to improve meant they seemed happy to keep coaching me.

When have you worked with someone wanting to change but needing to do so at their own pace?

How have you handled your own frustrations at them not changing in ways you'd expect, and how have you changed your own practice to work together cohesively?

When have you needed a coach or leader to understand how you learn and work most effectively, and how have you communicated that back to them?

If work really means something it's very motivational and maybe emotional

I worked with a group of Team Leaders once in a large UK power supply company. There were about 20 of us working in a room all day (I remember it well because it was a room with no natural light) and when we started discussing motivation we got talking about the value of having some kind of meaning in our work.

One of the Team Leaders was a well-built, broad, bald, tattooed man, maybe in his early 60s. He hadn't said much all day – not to the whole group at least – but the subject of having meaning in his work stirred him to speak.

He started to talk, slowly, about why he had joined the business many years before, and about the older or more vulnerable customers that relied on them to keep their homes warm during cold winters, and in some cases to stop people, literally, freezing to death. As he spoke his eyes became, maybe, just perceptibly watery, and the room was silent.

It was a powerful moment, and a real lesson for me in the

importance of being able to relate, in some way, to what you do. This team leader had a really clear picture of why his work was relevant for others, and for him.

There's an apocryphal story that you've probably heard about JFK visiting NASA back in the early 1960s. As JFK is shown round, he spies a man sweeping the floor and asks him what he is doing. The man sweeping says, "Mr President, I'm helping to put a man on the moon."

Whether your job is to help put a man on the moon or keep people warm, or even to help support people who enable something to happen that benefits people, it's good to be reminded of it regularly.

One of the most common things people say when I talk to them about what is important in their jobs, is to go out and talk to the people that use or benefit from your work, even if indirectly. Learning their stories and how your work helps makes a big difference when work seems challenging.

Why do you do what you do?

Who does it benefit, and what does knowing that mean to you?

Take care messing with motives

I can't remember where I first heard the story of the retired professor.

He was recently retired and looking forward to a peaceful summer, when a group of youths started to gather each night under the streetlight right outside his house. They would kick a ball about, shout, swear, leave rubbish and were generally a nuisance to someone like him after a quiet life.

After a few days he went out to talk to them. Rather than rant or moan he explained that before the group of lads turned up there had been a particularly nasty gang hanging around that spot. But since the lads had been there the nasty lot hadn't shown up once. So he asked the group of lads if he could pay them to keep coming. Surprised but happy, thinking the professor was nuts, they said yes.

Only the professor had a plan. After a while, he explained to them that since he was retired he couldn't afford to keep paying every night so reluctantly he was going to have to reduce the amount. The lads accepted but looked forward to coming each night to collect their (now slightly less) money. The professor repeated the conversation and, after the third payment reduction, the lads decided it wasn't worth their while to keep coming and cleared off somewhere else.

Money can really mess with motivation. Take care.

I've mentioned earlier that I have two cats, and one of them is probably too smart for his own good. If he is particularly hungry when my alarm goes off and I don't seem to be getting up and offering food quickly enough, he will pick a fight with his brother, knowing that hearing the two of them hissing and growling at each other (and occasionally pained meows) will get me out of bed to separate them! And once I'm up, he's more likely to get food which seems to be worth any risk that accompanies picking a fight.

Of course, the best way for me to respond would be to ignore them, which sometimes works, but it tends to be less annoying to stop the fight and deal with the problem.

What motivates you when it shouldn't?

How do you deal with other people (or animals) trying to motivate you, however blunt the manner?

And how do you try and motivate others? What works?

Be careful using money as an extra motivator

As mentioned elsewhere, I used to run a boys' football team. I started doing it when my son was about 8 and they needed a parent to come forward and manage the side.

One day, when they were not much older than that, and playing friendly games against other local sides, one of the other dads told me that he had said to his son that he would pay him £1 for every goal he scored. He seemed rather pleased with himself for the idea and the generosity.

But I wasn't so sure.

I asked the dad, politely I hope, why he would pay his boy to do something that the boy wanted to do anyway?!? And what would happen if the boy took a shot when it would be better for the team if he passed to another player? Or what he would do if the boy asked for £2 for each goal. Or what would happen to the boy's motivation when he stopped paying him. (I'm not sure in reality I asked all those questions. I probably just said "What on earth have you done that for?)

I think paying someone to do something that they want to do anyway needs careful consideration, and perhaps a discussion with that person first.

Money is a fascinating motivator. I've often had people tell me I should become a professional photographer or writer. Despite not being talented enough in crowded fields, it's something I've always responded to by saying that if I had to do it for money, I might not enjoy it as much and I didn't want to lose a hobby.

Many people who change their hobby into their job find that they no longer enjoy the thing they loved so much they chose to do it full-time, because the stress and pressure involved squash their creativity.

Research has shown that whilst earning money can be an important motivator, once someone achieves a certain salary level their motivation and satisfaction does not increase proportionally with any pay increase beyond that level.

What motivates you at work, or to do your hobby?

Does money change your motivation? How important is it compared to enjoying your work, or wanting to make a difference?

Staying motivated - signing up each year

In many professional sports the effort, focus and dedication required to be successful is enormous. Whether looking to earn enough to live on or to be rich, there are no half measures. If you're in an Olympic sport then the Olympics is the pinnacle of what you do. In some cases sports people and athletes have to consider if they are going to sign up - to commit - to the next four years of an Olympic cycle.

For many employees in organisations, contracts are permanent, and so this 're-signing up' doesn't take place. This is good, in reducing uncertainty and stress by providing stability and reassurance.

However it can mean that one year can roll into the next, without the mental commitment to sign up to meet the organisational challenges of the next 12 months. I wouldn't suggest making this a formal "signing up", but a periodic conversation - that checks in on what is going to be needed and the commitment to want to keep going - I think is a really useful thing.

"You have a permanent contract, but we'll check in on that each year (if not much more frequently) to talk about what we still need from you and that you still want to be here..."

(Could work for marriages too?)

When I first worked in a permanent office job, I remember a colleague being very nervous ahead of her annual review. I was a bit perplexed about why she was nervous given she seemed to do a great job and wasn't in any kind of trouble.

Although experience has allowed me to understand why she might have felt that way despite being a high performer, it does always seem odd to me when annual reviews are used to tick boxes or surprise people, rather than as an opportunity to offer praise and to get excited about what is coming up in the next year.

> How do you re-commit to your job?
>
> What gets you excited about the challenges ahead?
>
> How do you have conversations about your needs and what you can offer?

Motivation moves and fluctuates

I started a part-time Masters in about 2008, 20 years after my first degree. I was dead keen.

Initially I attended lectures one day a week during term time for two years whilst completing six modules. It was about an hour commute each way and was great – I learned some things, I learned some things I could apply in my work and I met some interesting people. These were three of my four reasons for doing the course.

The final element of the course was a dissertation but, 18 months after starting it, having issued and collected questionnaires, done some follow up interviews, and transcribed them, I found myself really struggling to get it finished. I had a lot going on at home at the time and I had just started telling a couple of people that I didn't think I was going to complete it.

Given that the dissertation itself was all about motivation the irony was not lost on me.

Having the actual qualification was my fourth reason for doing the course. But it was getting harder and harder to do the write up. I would do some work for a few hours then leave it for a few weeks and each time I picked it up it would take me ages to get back up to speed with where I was before progressing it.

Then two things happened. A customer told me a friend of his had been made redundant and was thinking of doing a masters in applied sports psychology, just like me, and asked if I would chat to him. I said yes, of course, but inside I felt a bit of a fraud.

Secondly, a young lady, Anna, joined the business I was working in straight from Uni with a masters in sports psychology. Ouch, that hurt. And I suddenly felt like I was slipping behind.

The masters had a 5-year deadline for total completion and eventually I got over the line - just - more relieved to pass than anything else.

The reason for the story is to illustrate how tricky and slippery motivation can be. Did I motivate myself to pass? Was Anna's appearance just the luck I needed? Did I use my knowledge of motivation to help (no, I don't think so, I think it just happened).

Motivation is a funny old thing. If I try and explain what happened now, I think Anna joining made me feel out of control, and I wanted to feel more in control, and this, together with the deadline, was the impetus I needed to get on with it.

Sometimes serendipity undoubtedly plays a part.

When I started working on writing these stories down, I thought I'd be able to get them done and dusted in a few hours. It meant that I put off doing them because I'd be able to polish the task off quickly. When I did come to spend a few hours on them, it became apparent that I wouldn't be able to finish it in one go!

After a while of feeling I needed to spend a few hours at a time on writing or it wouldn't be worthwhile, I realised that spending an hour every weekend, which was about five stories, give or take, was the best way to motivate myself to get them written.

An hour at a time didn't feel like a big ask, or a lot out of my weekend, and if I had other things on that meant I couldn't manage an hour, catching up an extra five stories the following week might not be too hard. It has meant it has taken me a lot longer than I'd hoped to get this far, but I've also enjoyed making steady progress each week!

What do you use to motivate yourself with tasks that feel out of your control?

Does breaking things down into achievable parts help you to 'eat the elephant'? Or do you need an external deadline, or even someone else making you feel a bit less in control than you had thought?

The difference in saying it out loud to someone else

I worked with a group of people once on a programme where I was the performance coach. As part of this I also coached each individual 1-1. With one person, after a couple of the group sessions, in our first 1-1, we got talking about the importance of physical energy.

I broached the subject of this person's weight. They were youngish (early 30s?), successful in work and popular, but also obese. I can't remember exactly what enabled me to broach the subject. I remember feeling I was taking a risk, that I might offend them in some way.

They explained their story, of how they had essentially lost control of their eating and drinking habits, and their weight. It was complicated with multiple factors involved but when we started talking about the potential life consequences (life threatening consequences) for them, we both got a bit emotional. I don't think the person had ever had that conversation with someone else before.

I think saying it out loud made a big difference. Together with me the person made a plan, to start, to make some lifestyle decisions and to make some changes – involving multiple inputs.

Looking back now there was some bravery involved, by both of us, some honesty and some very practical steps too.

Whether it is having a problem with food, alcohol, gambling, or drugs, any of the addictions that society seems to enable but also disapprove of are very hard to talk about, especially without judgement. Family and friends can often feel too close to a problem or too judgemental to open up to when it comes to difficult situations. A lot of people find it far easier to point a finger at someone who has a problem, or be abusive, rather than let them explore what is going wrong.

Finding a neutral person can make it much easier to open up about a problem, but speaking it out loud for the first time can be incredibly difficult. Finding the bravery to speak about it often only happens when the person we're talking to has made it clear that they're not going to pass judgement or tell us what we should do. Once we trust them to be helpful and supportive, taking that big first step can be a lot easier but still requires a lot.

What happens when you find someone you trust to open up to?

How is it most helpful for them to respond to your vulnerability?

How do you respond if someone shares something important with you and allows you to see their fears and weaknesses?

Mastery and ego – focus on mastery

I can't remember when I first heard about mastery and ego orientations. But I definitely recall learning about it on a course at the same time as I was the manager of the local junior boys' football team.

Learning about it helped me understand myself better and my motivations.

Broadly, a person with a high ego orientation wants to win. Success is doing better than others. A person with a high mastery orientation wants to get better at the task. Success is improvement and being better than they were before. People can be highly motivated by one, or other, or both or neither.

To test this I organised a sprint at the end of the boys' football training. I instructed then to line up on one touchline and told them that when I said "go" we were going to have a sprint to the other side. I deliberately avoided saying it was a race.

When I said "go" I observed many things:

- Some boys immediately ran like it was a race. They wanted to win or beat as many others as possible
- Of those boys, one or two, when they realised they weren't going to win, reduced their effort or gave up
- Others realised they weren't going to win but kept going their hardest anyway
- Others knew before the start that they weren't going to win but ran their hardest anyway, trying throughout to get across the pitch as fast as they possibly could
- And one or two weren't bothered. Maybe they were tired at the end of training but they just jogged or walked across

Both motivations can be helpful. But with care! Ego motivation can lead to lots of comparisons, maybe a drop in motivation when realising others are better, or burnout and breakdown if driving yourself too long and too hard.

Mastery, or task motivation, tends to have less downsides, though those with perfectionist tendencies might still find themselves driving themselves in an unhelpful, or unhealthy way.

I've been thinking about the two ego orientations Jim mentions, and I wondered if there are other motivations. I was wondering because I'd been thinking about curiosity and eagerness to learn, where people are motivated to explore the world because they are fascinated by it. Does that count as high mastery – wanting to be better? Maybe. I suppose in some people it might also be high ego – that knowing more is equivalent to success. But maybe it is an alternative driver that fits neither box.

I also wondered how you tell whether the people around you – or even yourself – are motivated by ego or mastery at any one time? Some people will be fairly obvious, but they might not always be driven by the same things depending on the circumstances. And some people might have very different drivers every time.

How would you respond to that if you were a manager, coach or leader?

What about as a friend or family member?

We are all different and respond differently to different things – not everyone is like you

While there might be some general truths about the way we are motivated (or the things that motivate us) we are all different.

Motivational theories include things like mastery and ego; needs for achievement vs fear of failure: goal theory; intrinsic vs extrinsic and, from self-determination theory, autonomy, competence, and relatedness.

It's all too easy to assume that others are motivated by the same things and in the same way as us. Combine that with scenarios where a leader, manager or parent is frustrated (by someone else's inaction or inability) and it's no wonder that interactions are not always helpful!

A friend of mine gives a good example. He used to play professional football and following a change of management at his boyhood club, where he was struggling to regularly command a first team place, he made the brave decision to move elsewhere.

At his new club a combination of things, including injury and a change of management there, made life pretty challenging.

In one particular game my friend, a quiet chap, technically strong, not the biggest, was not having his best game. Coming into the changing room at half time he knew he had not been playing well.

What he probably needed was an arm round the shoulder. And a quiet word in his ear about what a great player he was - something to keep his confidence high and to encourage him to keep going, and to try things.

Instead, he got a punch in the face. Literally. In some way this was meant to help. The effect it had was to completely shock my friend. In the second half he said he was physically on the pitch but mentally somewhere else, like Timbuktu.

Thankfully in most workplaces HR practice means that that type of behaviour would be a case for dismissal. And most (most!) managers have got a bit more sensitivity.

But it's a good example of how wrong people can get it! We are all different and respond to different things.

Going into my second year at university after spending the first playing rugby almost constantly, I expected to have a similar experience. However, the university team had a new coach and captain, the latter having taken my position and I hadn't quite realised that meant I would have to find a new place in the team.

For the first game of the season, they decided to play me in the second row of the scrum, despite me having no experience playing there and telling the coach and captain that. It's a pretty important position to get technically correct, and I really struggled to make things work. The whole scrum was very unstable during the game, no matter what I tried, giving our opponents a significant advantage. I offered to move to a position that I was more experienced in, either in the front row or the back row, but the captain and the other players just yelled at me for not getting it right, and the coach joined in from the sidelines.

At the end of the game I walked off, collected my belongings and went home without even showering. I didn't play rugby again for another year. Being shouted at didn't help me solve the problems I was facing, and I didn't want to be part of a team that thought that was an appropriate response to someone being out of their depth.

Reading the story of Jim's friend, I was lucky that I wasn't punched in the face!

What is the worst situation you've been in where you have needed support or encouragement and didn't get it?

How did you respond?

How has that changed how you support those around you?

---

6 GOALS AND TARGETS

"The greatest danger for most of us is not that our aim is too high and we miss it, but it is too low and we reach it."

MICHELANGELO

"Would you tell me please. Which way I ought to go from here?"

"That depends a good deal on where you want to get to", said the cat.

"I don't much care where", said Alice.

"Then it doesn't matter which way you go", said the cat.

ALICE IN WONDERLAND, LEWIS CARROLL

"If you want to make God laugh, tell him your plans."

WOODY ALLEN

As I write I remind myself that people can lead incredibly satisfying, worthwhile or successful lives without ever having goals or targets. At the same time, there is no doubt that used well in the right circumstances, they can be highly motivational.

The textbook will tell you that goals give a sense of direction, give you something to review against, help you overcome obstacles and learn/adapt when you are not on track.

In the world of work and life I see goals as tools. Something to use rather than just have.

The skill of using gold, silver and bronze goals

For several years I coached a junior football team. We had enough players for two teams of 11 and when they were young we always just picked two even teams. Players develop physically, tactically and mentally at such different times and it never seemed the right thing to start labelling anyone as better or worse than anyone else.

By the time the boys reached about 11, or first year of secondary school in the UK, we decided it was time to have an A and B team by ability (by now the boys could see how good each other was and the squads pretty much picked themselves anyway).

One of my fellow parent coaches was an ex-professional player and qualified coach and he took the A team. I was very happy to take the B team boys.

That season the second team lost their first game and kept losing.

We lost every game in the first half of the season. Even though I was very aware that the boys played for lots of reasons - to be with mates, to have fun, to score goals, to run around, to try hard, and more (and, 5 minutes after each defeat, they had usually forgotten the score anyway) the game still exists to win, and as coach, even I was getting the teeniest bit bothered at losing every single week.

So I had an idea and suggested to the boys that, in the second half of the season, we try and improve our score against each team. I told them that I had kept the score against each team and that we could aim to improve each time. The boys liked the idea and I gave myself a pat on the back.

Unfortunately, the next game, the first in the second half of the season, was against the team we had lost to in the opening game.

We had lost 2-1 and since then, while we had lost every week, they were now unbeaten and topped the league. Added to that we only had 10 players so to improve on a 2-1 defeat seemed very unlikely.

We needed a new plan.

I had been introduced to the idea of Gold, Silver and Bronze medal goals (or targets) and had used them myself or with others many times.

I decided to use gold, silver, bronze goals and I introduced them to the boys. I explained that a bronze medal was the minimum that we would be happy with, that a silver medal would represent something pretty good and that a gold medal would represent something special - a fantastic achievement that didn't come around very often.

I started by asking them, as a team, what would be their gold medal for the game today?

"To win", several of them said.

I felt this was highly unlikely. Impossibly so. I pointed out that we hadn't won all season, that we were playing the team at the top of the league, and we were a player short.

Someone said "to draw the game" and even though I felt that was also pretty impossible we settled on that. This was a gold medal after all and gold medals don't come very easily.

"What would be a silver medal?" I asked next. There was some discussion and we settled on "to lose by four goals or less". We had had some real drubbings so this seemed like a good silver medal target.

Finally, I asked, "what would be a good bronze medal target for us today?" There was a lot of discussion and eventually, with just about no input from me, the boys decided it was two things. Firstly, to keep trying throughout the whole game and, secondly, to not get cross with each other.

I thought these were fantastic because a) the boys had come up with them by themselves and b) because this target was in our own hands, in our control.

At half time, playing into the wind, we were losing 4-0. The boys came off the pitch looking a little dejected. I tried to raise the spirits by reminding them that we were on target for a silver medal and this seemed to help (they were too young or tired or incapable of extrapolating to work out this would mean 8-0 at full time).

In the second half we managed a rare attack into the opponent's half of the pitch and won a corner. One of the boys trotted off in the far distance to take it. They were still small boys and it was a big distance from corner flag to the goal.

The corner was taken and the ball came across in front of the goal and bounced past everyone until it got to a young lad on our team, Joe. Joe couldn't really kick a ball very well. But on this occasion the ball hit Joe's swinging leg on the shin and went in.

There were big celebrations. We rarely scored.

We were now losing 4-1 and, in all my time watching and playing team sport, I've never seen a team work as hard as they did for the rest of the match.

The game finished 4-1 and it felt like we had won the Olympics, never mind a silver medal.

Happy days.

The idea of setting gold, silver and bronze goals - rather than a binary hit or not hit the goal - is a simple and powerful one.

I can be pretty terrible at setting achievable goals for myself. I get excited about big ideas and try and achieve whole projects in one go – and then get disheartened when I can't do it. An idea that is a good idea surely shouldn't take long, right?

When Jim first introduced me to the idea of tiered goal-setting using gold, silver, and bronze as targets, it really helped me accept that success isn't always black and white, or that I have to finish every big thing on the first go. When I get to the end of the week and reflect on what I have achieved, I try to consider whether the week has been one where I have overachieved (gold), achieved everything I needed to (silver), or had some setbacks but still managed to make progress (bronze). That in itself can make it easier to step away from work on a Friday evening, rather than trying to persevere until I am too tired to continue.

How do you set goals and judge your success?

What do you take into account when you reflect on the week, and how does that help you leave work behind you for the weekend?

An example of how tiered goals helped a record-breaking swim

I used gold, silver and bronze goals when helping Dom Boon prepare for a swimming challenge he'd taken on. Already an experienced open water swimmer Dom decided to take on the swim from Europe to North Africa across the Strait of Gibraltar. At 8.1 miles (13km) wide at its narrowest point the swim is especially hazardous because of the tides and shipping to contend with.

It was a big challenge for which he prepared hard and well.

Dom set himself gold, silver and bronze finish times and also made a detailed plan for both the run up to the day and the swim himself. He had a family member with him in a support boat.

He set gold, silver and bronze goals along the lines of:
- Bronze – follow my plan on the day – do the process
- Silver – do my plan and hit one of three target times (a gold/silver/bronze time)
- Gold – silver medal and enjoy the whole experience too

On the day, with great effort, he managed to deliver a gold – in what turned out to be a record-breaking swim. (As at 2023 he still holds the record.)

Having the three goals relieved some pressure and enabled him to target gold.

Back when I was at high school, we used to get sent out in pairs for 'cross-country' runs around a loop of local pavements and footpaths. It was all fairly flat and gentle, but as someone who was perennially unfit, completely uninterested in running, and in all likelihood dyspraxic and with undiagnosed mild asthma, it wasn't something that I saw the point of at all. As soon as I was out of sight of the teachers, I would walk the course as much as my running partner would allow – and of course, I usually ended up going with someone else who was as enthusiastic about the situation as I was. I knew I risked getting into trouble, but I couldn't see any benefit to the discomfort and pain of the run which was far worse for me than any punishment the teachers could mete out.

One day, the teachers asked us to really give it our best shot and for some unknown reason, I decided to try a bit harder than usual. Although I didn't run all the way, I knocked several minutes off my usual time.

It would have been really helpful to have tiered goals in that situation; mixing running and walking like a couch-to-5k programme, or setting timed goals to aim towards. I'm pretty competitive, so even though I hated running, I probably would have gone for it if I had something realistic - for me - to aim for.

When would tiered goals have helped you improve or achieve something new?

How could you use them to do something that you're proud of, even in difficult circumstances?

Extreme conditions might mean adjusting your goals and getting a better outcome

I've never run the London marathon but I did go and watch it once. My younger brother Matt was running it, so as a family we went to support. I decided to go with him to the start before meeting up with the others later to watch him on the route.

It was an early start, but by the time we gathered with the thousands of others at his assembly point, there was already warmth in the blue April sky. At one point while wandering around, we passed someone, very prepared, putting some sun cream on the back of their neck and I remember saying to him later that if we saw anyone else doing that we might cadge some off them.

It turned out to be an abnormally hot spring day.

The race was sponsored by Aqua Pura and afterwards the story went around that some water stations had run out. When we met my brother at about the 18-mile mark, where they came back into central London from the fairly barren Isle of Dogs (at that time, the mid 1990s, parts of it were bleak), he was in a bad way.

He shouldn't really have been running at all having been ill with bronchitis about six weeks before – but he was keen to take part having done so much training. We bought him a bottle of water from a local garage and he managed to walk and jog to the finish.

It turns out that a temperature of 22.7C (72.8F) was recorded at St James's Park that day. Compare this to the average of 15.0C for that date in April and that all his training would have taken place in average temperatures lower than that.

Wind the clock forward 22 years to 2018. I knew three people, all coaching customers, taking part that year. All were well sponsored and wanted to run a good time too. However the temperature that day turned out to be a new record high at a whopping 24.1C (75.3F), again recorded in St James's Park.

It turned out that the three had very different experiences.

One made no particular adjustment for the conditions, another decided that his bronze medal target time before the day was now his gold and the third decided that all bets were off, times were out of the window and he was just going to aim to run around and enjoy it.

Well, the first guy blew up, got overcooked and finished hours, literally, outside his original target times. The second guy finished outside his new gold target. And the third guy was pretty pleased with his run and was very satisfied with how it had gone.

Goals are something to aim for, but not always something to carve in stone (despite what people always say about never giving up).

When I was in my first year at university, I played a lot of rugby. My family joked that I was studying rugby, not history! Between the university team and the local club, Tuesdays were my only day away from playing or training. Towards the end of the season, I broke a metacarpal in my hand during a game and was out for a month or so. Desperate to get back to playing as soon as I could, I started spending time in the gym to try and improve my fitness while my hand healed. One of the gym staff was an England Academy rugby player, and encouraged by my commitment in the gym, suggested I go to England open trials that summer.

Spurred on by the new goal, I kept at it in the gym, even after my exams were over. A few weeks before the trials, I went with the club team to play at the national Sevens tournament over a long weekend. The England Academy player joined us for the weekend, and I felt it was a great opportunity to get back into the swing of game situations ahead of the trials.

Unfortunately, and I have no idea why, I had absolutely nothing in the tank that weekend. Despite all the gym work, I was walking around the pitches feeling like I was wearing lead boots. The England Academy player and I had a brief conversation, agreeing that I shouldn't go to trials.

Although I was disappointed, I was glad to have had the chance to discover that I wasn't going to succeed at the trials before I went and potentially embarrassed myself. Whilst it was painful to give up on the dream of playing a higher level of rugby, it was the right decision and one I've never regretted.

When have you had to confront an unexpected reality, and adjust your goals because things didn't work out as planned?

How did you cope with that change, and would you do things differently in hindsight?

Knowing the environment can be extremely helpful

I remember hearing Serena Williams talk about how much she loves Wimbledon. Not surprising since she has won the ladies singles title there seven times!

In the interview I heard I remember her saying two things about her knowledge of her surroundings that were helping her to be her best.

Traveling away from home as a professional sportsperson goes with the territory but is still another challenge to be dealt with. Another hotel room, more optimum food choices to arrange, how and where to relax. Serena explained that at Wimbledon she knew the area and had found a great private guest house to rent out that made life so much easier.

Secondly, she knew the tennis facility well and many of the people who worked there year after year at the tournament. If she was ever hanging around before practice or matches, and she wanted a quiet space to chill, she knew places to go.

These might seem like little things but "local knowledge" however gained, can be invaluable. Whether this comes from experience or by sussing things out ahead of time. As the military expression goes, "time spent on reconnaissance is seldom wasted".

One of the things I used to really enjoy doing during my time off was to go out and about with my camera. I love landscape shots and a friend recommended a really helpful app called 'The Photographer's Ephemeris' – a map that allows you pinpoint any location, on any day, and see the line of sunrise, sunset, moonrise and so on from that point.

A couple of years ago, I had some time off just before Christmas and decided that as the weather was good, I would go into London and take some photos. After a little while wandering around the Millennium Bridge and St Paul's under beautiful blue skies, I met a friend for lunch. Afterwards, she had a little time and I said that if she came with me, I could pretty much guarantee a good view of the sunset. So we wandered down to Embankment tube, picked up a coffee, and then went onto the footbridges overlooking the Thames and the Houses of Parliament. We timed it almost perfectly, and just as I was starting to feel I'd overpromised, the sun suddenly lit up the clouds over Westminster and the river before fading quickly into a dark December night.

Although I got a bit lucky with the sky deciding to perform (never a given), the time that I'd spent beforehand in working out where I might get the most picturesque sunset paid off. Of course, it doesn't always work out quite so well in practice; a year or two after that trip, the app told me that the line of sunset would be roughly through Tower Bridge in late March before the clocks changed, about an hour or so after I finished work in central London. I planned my trip carefully, went over after work, and discovered that due to various buildings being in the way and there only being a limited number of vantage points to stand on the riverside looking back through the bridge, I couldn't quite get the shots I'd envisioned. I still got some wonderful shots which I'm very proud of, but it was one time where my preparation didn't quite go as planned!

When have you found that doing a bit of groundwork has really helped you succeed?

When could you do a bit more reconnaissance to really make things go smoothly?

Reducing pressure and stress by adjusting the goal

I once knew a young man who worked in the same office as me. He was personable, likeable, hardworking, good at his job, a leader of his team and someone always looking to do better.

One day he explained to me that he was going to start doing some professional exams and asked me if I would be his mentor. Flattered, I said yes, though I wasn't too sure what I would bring. True, I had successfully studied for and passed quite a few exams, including while working full time.

Some months later, this chap - who was now onto module two - asked if he could have a word. He explained that he was struggling with everything that was happening. Work was busy, and he had recently become a Dad, so everything was pretty full on. He wasn't sure if he was going to be able to continue the study.

"Hmmm", I said. "That sounds tough". (I think I said something like this, but I'm probably telling this story in my favour, I'm not that naturally empathetic). "Tell me", I continued, "what mark did you get in your first module?"

"94%" he replied. I already knew the answer because he had told me before.

"And what is the pass mark?" I asked.

"40%" he answered.

"Ah", I said, and paused (cleverly).

"Ah!" he said. "I see what you mean".

We don't always have the option to reduce the goal or target to make life a little easier when we're struggling, but sometimes we do. And sometimes that's ok, either temporarily or more long-term.

When I was finishing my undergraduate degree, I took what was called a 'special subject' – an in-depth double-weighted course that spanned the full final year and counted for half of the year's marks. There were specific rules around what could be included in the final examination at the end of the year and which parts were only assessed by coursework. When the final exams were looming, the course cohort reached out to our slightly eccentric lecturer for some revision advice.

He called us all to his study early one morning, told us he couldn't remember which parts of the course he'd included in the exam and that he hadn't paid any attention to the rules around what could and could not be included, and then berated us for asking him questions. After this performance, one of the other students said that he would give it his best shot but wasn't too concerned as he felt that his grades were good enough across several other modules to get at least a 2:1, if not a first, via the university's preponderance method. This rule meant that if a student had received a certain grade across half or more of their modules in their final two years, they would receive that grade regardless of what they had scored in the remaining modules.

The lecturer had not been aware of this rule; he exclaimed it preposterous and accused the student in question of being lazy, cynical and a cheat – or words to that effect. He threatened to check it all with the university and the school of history as it couldn't possibly be an acceptable way to get a final degree grade! Yet of course it was correct and my fellow student was right to be so pragmatic as the final exam was pretty painful.

In this instance, my fellow student was taking a realistic approach at a difficult time. If this particular exam was going to be impossible to prepare for, he would do his best but not let it distract him from preparing for his other more predictable exams which were just as important to his final grade. He knew he had enough leeway from his existing hard work to mean that something really unexpected in the final exam wouldn't ruin his chances of the grade he was aiming for.

> When have you had to take a pragmatic approach to your goals?
>
> What helped you make that decision, and how did you feel about it? Did it help?

Perspective makes a difference to the outcomes you are after

Sometime after university I was job hunting. I had a couple of periods of looking. One was right after I had finished my PGCE but had decided teaching was not for me. I ended up getting a job in sports administration through a friend of mine.

The other time was a couple of years later. That first job had come to end, and I was doing various temporary jobs to pay the rent. I was signed on for a few weeks at about that time too.

At one point I was applying for some graduate jobs, not knowing what my chances were. So I was delighted to get a reply asking me to attend an assessment centre.

A week or two later I got a letter saying that they were sorry, but the graduate scheme was not happening that year and the assessments would not take place.

I was disappointed and a bit angry. I felt let down. Having calmed down, and talked to my Mum, I decided to ring them. I thought it would at least help to get my frustration off my chest.

As soon as the lady answered the phone things changed. Before I could say much she told me, very genuinely, how terribly sorry they were and how the company decision to not take on graduates that year meant she and her colleague would in all likelihood lose their jobs. Talk about having the wind taken out of your sails.

Suddenly my position was totally different. This lady was about to join me amongst the unemployed.

Situations and perspectives can change very quickly. Sometimes all you can do is accept something, dust yourself down, learn any lessons and go again.

When I was very small, we had two lovely cats, Chaka and Sheba. My parents had got them a few years before my brother and I arrived on the scene, and they did very well to endure two boisterous toddlers – and a few years after this story, my little sister's arrival too. I absolutely adored the cats but as a fairly excitable small child, I rarely managed to approach them in a way that didn't scare them off.

One day when I was three or four, my Dad explained to me that they were frightened of me because I was so much bigger than them. He had me lie on the floor, and then stood next to me to show me how big and intimidating I must have appeared to the cats, and that because I was so much bigger than them I had to slow down when approaching them.

His advice must have worked because as I got a bit older, they became much more comfortable with me and would sleep on my bed. I've never forgotten the power of that lesson and how taking a cat's-height perspective on humans was so helpful in understanding what I needed to do.

It's a much more literal take on perspective than Jim's story!

When have you found that taking a bit of perspective has helped you?

What did you change as a result?

7 MASTERY AND CONFIDENCE

"The big thing I've learned is to ease back before races. I don't panic. I have confidence. I don't see any reason why I shouldn't win."

PAULA RADCLIFFE,

one month after breaking the world record.

"So I was getting into my car, and this bloke says to me, "Can you give me a lift?". I said "Sure, you look great, the world's your oyster, go for it."

TOMMY COOPER

In all my coaching conversations, the topic that comes up most often – in some form or other – is confidence. Confidence itself is a slippery character. It can rise and fall, it can feel solid and elusive and whilst high confidence can be achieved, it's rarely totally within one's control.

Confidence makes a tremendous difference. When added to skill the two combine very powerfully. And confidence can, at times in certain situations, make up for a lack of skill in remarkable ways.

I love the first story in this section for the absurd illogic it brings to something that some would say is a science. I'm not so sure.

The mindset of a basketball shooter and what we can learn from it

I love the following story, quoted from a Bob Rotella book, because of the stunning simplicity of the thinking. For me and for others, this story has either provided a light bulb moment or has reinforced something that they perhaps thought they already knew but weren't sure.

The story is relevant for people who perhaps have experienced self-doubt or wondered how more confident people might think (to overcome their more negative experiences or help them get in a more helpful mindset). This is a very common challenge and scenario.

The story illustrates how helpful thinking helps maximise talent - talent that is also being developed through the hard work and practice that is required for consistent performance, such as that of successful basketball shooter or a successful golfer.

From Golf Is Not A Game Of Perfect, by Dr Bob Rotella

"...Stuart Anderson, (was) a University of Virginia football player who went on to play for several years with the Washington Redskins. Stuart took a seminar I gave on confidence in athletics. I asked him to share with the class what went through his mind when he was thinking confidently.

Stuart replied with a story from his high-school basketball career.

"I was a fifty percent shooter from the floor," he said. "In the first round of the state play offs during my senior year I took my first shot and missed."

Stuart kept missing. He had the worst shooting night of his life in that game. He missed twenty-odd shots in a row. His team teetered on the edge of elimination.

One of the other students in the seminar asked, "Stuart, why didn't you start passing the ball after you missed, say, ten in a row?"

"Because I'm a shooter. But let me finish the story," Stuart said.

His team scrapped and stayed in the game. With a minute to go, trailing by a point, they stole the ball and called time out. The coach, reasoning that Stuart was irremediably cold that night, diagrammed a play to run 55 seconds off the clock and set up a shot for another player, a junior.

"Wait a minute, Coach!" Stuart objected. I want the shot. Give me the ball!"

The underclassman, it turned out, didn't really want the shot at that stage. So the coach, against his better judgement, changed his plan and called a play to give Stuart the shot.

He got the ball beside the free throw line, one of his favourite spots. He turned and jumped, absolutely confident. His eyes zeroed in on the rim. He let the shot go.

And in it went. Stuart was the hero. Fans carried him off the floor. The next day, the newspapers headlined his game-winning shot.

After hearing this story, one of my students raised a hand and asked, "How did you stay so confident after you missed all those shots?"

"Well, you have to understand. I've always been a fifty percent shooter," Stuart replied. "After I missed one, I figured the next one was likely to go in. After I missed two, I was overdue. By the time I'd missed five, I figured the next one absolutely had to drop. Every time I missed, I figured the odds were increasing in my favour."

"Okay," the student said. "If that's how you think when you miss your first shots, what do you think if you make your first six or seven in a row?"

"That's totally different," Stuart said. "You decide that tonight's your night, you're on a hot streak, and you're going to make everything you look at."

"That's ridiculous," the student said. "You can't have it both ways."

"Of course you can", Stuart said.

Stuart had revealed something very basic about the way good athletes think. They create their own realities. They think however they need to think to maintain their confidence and get the job done. In basketball this is called the shooter's mentality.

This may seem, to an outsider, to be absolutely irrational. How can a kid who's just missed twenty-odd shots in a row be confident he's going to make the next one?

The answer is that whether it's irrational or not, it's more effective than the alternative."

Our thinking can and does make a difference to how we feel and behave. I think that kind of helpful thinking can be learned - by trial and error, or by learning from others - but can also be speeded up with some deliberate learning and practice.

I have a weird aversion. It's something that really confuses pretty much everyone I encounter who I have to explain it to, but it's always been a part of my life. I have a phobia of milk. I don't like to look at it, and I never consume it. I don't even drink anything with milk in the name, or coffee with milk in. I don't eat cereal because it's pretty disappointing eating it dry.

As I mentioned, this confounds a lot of people; I remember a particular incident at a dinner where I'd explained this in advance and asked for a sauce on the menu to be omitted from my plate. The wait staff were particularly perplexed when they served me dessert and I complained because my plate didn't have the scoop of ice-cream that everyone else's did. Explaining that ice-cream is different because it's solid didn't seem to make any sense to them.

I've discovered over time that as long as I don't see the milk in something, or it doesn't look creamy, I can sometimes trick myself into not acknowledging that something has milk in and eating it. It's not easy to explain to other people, and - as happened once - if someone were to point out to me while I was drinking hot chocolate that it is just hot milk with a bit of chocolate, I wouldn't be able to drink it. In the same way I couldn't eat pasta with carbonara sauce, but I could manage lasagne if I mixed the ragu and cheese sauce together so that the white sauce wasn't white.

Weird? Yep.

Completely contradictory? Absolutely.

Silly example? Probably.

However, whilst this example of being able to hold two simultaneous and contradictory beliefs is a little daft, it goes to show that our minds are remarkable in being able to find ways around ourselves, once we work out how to do it.

How often have you had to hold contradictory beliefs in order to get the best possible result? And how have you managed the contradiction?

What stories have you told yourself to find that optimal course?

Valuing your own experience in order to build your confidence

Many years ago I did a temporary job during a gap year. (It was so long ago the phrase gap year didn't exist. Back then it was a 'year out'). I worked for the TSB - the Trustee Savings Bank - at their new Unit Trust headquarters just outside the town centre in Andover. The job was in a kind of garage, and one part of it included getting company cars ready for each fresh crop of suited and booted salespeople. It was so 1980s.

There was an old chap working there who also played the trumpet in the Salvation Army band. I remember him once talking to me about what a long time he had been playing, and also about young trumpeters who would come along to the band. He also told me - quite matter-of-factly, not boastfully - that he was kind of uplifted by the thought that those youngsters, just taking up the trumpet, would never be as good as him. His lifetime of playing and practicing meant that for as long as he was still playing, he couldn't be caught up by them.

He really believed in the value of all his years of practicing and playing.

Many jobs have some similarities, including coaching. Whatever we do we all have plenty to continue to learn, refine and adopt. But at the same time one's lifetime experience is something that can't be bought. It has to be... experienced.

And that can be a great source of confidence, when you get there.

As I've mentioned earlier, I'm quite into photography as a hobby. I'm a member of a couple of Facebook groups where people share their shots, and sometimes arrange days out together. It can be really inspiring to see people who are more experienced and better than you, and learn from them how they made the shot happen. Sometimes it can also be a bit intimidating, as you look at phenomenal compositions and feel like you're never going to have that sort of eye for a shot, or the ability and desire to get up in the dark in winter and go out with the camera on the off chance of something good...

What's great about these groups is that they welcome everyone, and so you also get to see shots from people who perhaps don't have as much expertise and experience as you have built up. And you can look at their shots and think "Ah, but I would have done this, or cropped that, to improve this shot." And although you would never tell them that you think their shot could be improved, it reminds you of how far you've come in your own photography journey. In the same way, sometimes I look back at old photographs, and wonder why on earth I thought they were any good.

What gives you perspective and allows you to see how far you've come and how experienced you are?

What prompts you to reflect on your own expertise?

Take care not to convince yourself you can't do things you can

I was once at a sales conference where Dave Alred was the guest speaker. At the time I knew him to be Jonny Wilkinson's kicking coach.

He did a great exercise with the whole audience getting us to think about our capabilities, our mindset and how the way we think affects how we behave.

He asked everyone to stand up.

Then he said: "If you can play tennis, I want you to remain standing, but everyone else sit down".

The vast majority of people sat down. These were the people who I guess were thinking "I've never played", or "I can't play", or "I can play, but not very well", or "I'm rubbish" i.e. all those things we tell ourselves to protect ourselves, avoid embarrassment, to avoid being seen as big-headed, to avoid being in the spotlight.

Then he said: "If you can hold a tennis racket and hit a ball across a net stand back up". Almost everyone did.

He said "All of you standing up can play tennis".

Most of us in that room could play tennis, in some way, at some level. But most had sat down to start with.

The point I took away was that our minds can be our worst enemy. They can restrict us, tell us we can't do something, affect our confidence and a whole lot more.

But they can also be our greatest asset.

I was once chatting to someone who was concerned that because they had been doing their job for many years, the organisation would see them as expendable if they put a toe out of line, let alone a foot wrong. We discussed what it would look like to view their work through the perspective of someone more senior, and how that senior person would have to take a look at their long history of good performance and dedication to their work, and how that might mean this person and their hard work were far more valued than it perhaps felt like at times.

Sometimes it's helpful to frame your self-view differently in order to understand how good you are and build your confidence. We're all humans, and we need to believe that the things we spend our time on are worthwhile and that we are good at them. Without that, we don't feel much sense of purpose.

> What has helped you re-frame your perspective of your skills and expertise?
>
> What questions would you ask someone else to help them do the same?

The value of putting your name in the hat rather than talking yourself out of it

My first job after graduating was in a small office near Euston station in London as a sports administrator. I loved it. Unfortunately the office relocated to Birmingham and with it my job ended. Several temporary jobs came and went while I applied for dozens, literally, of sport related roles.

Eventually, looking for more security, I applied and got a graduate role with an insurance company, like you do. After the first two years, at the end of the graduate programme, I got my first permanent role there. After several months a job came up in HR which appealed, but which was well beyond my grade and experience. A colleague from the graduate scheme, Janet, and I discussed it as she was interested too. She applied and I didn't.

She wasn't offered the job but, the HR team liked her, and created an intermediate role for her in HR. I was hacked off at the time but only had myself to blame. I did resolve not to not put my hat in the ring again.

Sheryl Sandberg tells similar stories in her book Lean In when discussing the principle "Sit at the Table". Hers is a good read.

After my colleagues and I finished working with Jim on his high performance programme a few years ago, I got quite interested in coaching. I did some informal coaching with colleagues, and half-heartedly investigated getting a qualification but felt I couldn't really afford to do a course.

I had lunch with one of my cohort colleagues a few months after this, and she told me that she was going do a part-time masters in coaching to get qualified. I felt devastated that I wasn't doing that too as it was something that I'd love to do. As it happens, that level of study doesn't appeal to me but my friend successfully completed her course and now works as a coach in the specialism she had wanted to.

Like Jim, I only had myself to blame for not finding and taking the opportunity that I wanted to take, but I've also been happy to continue developing my career in other areas with a view to coming back to coaching in the future.

When have you felt jealous of someone else taking an opportunity that you would have liked but didn't go for?

How has that changed you?

Has it made you take more opportunities since then?

Be you

I worked for a couple of years as a Training & Development Consultant in a large company and was partnered with an office based sales function that grew to about 60 people.

This meant, along with sales managers and others, running induction programmes for new sales consultants as well as delivering ongoing training for all the people in the function. To practice customer call scenarios we would run roleplays where I would draft a brief to be played out.

Often the trainee consultant had a lot of new information to take in and learn, about products, about customers and about how to develop into an effective salesperson. And they were often a bit nervous too.

At the bottom of each roleplay brief, where the consultant was trying to absorb information, and think about their words and tactics, I would write the two words "Be you".

I believe we're often at our best when we're just being us. Obviously there are times where we want or need to be someone else – putting on an act – but by and large we do our best work when we are being us!

If I could give one bit of advice to the younger me it might well be "be you, more often".

I heard James Haskell, former international rugby player, in conversation with Annie Vernon, former international rower, talking about all the top-level coaches he had ever worked with and how one, the Australian Eddie Jones, was the best coach for him because he encouraged him to "be you".

Finally I remember being very struck by this quote from jazz musician Miles Davis "Man, sometimes it takes you a long time to sound like yourself."

Being you is not always that straightforward, but I think it's a journey of discovery that is rewarding, enlightening and fulfilling.

I worked with someone recently who always had something nice to say about you. What a trait to have! I think it was probably an approach that had been honed with practice, especially as it always came across as heartfelt and genuine.

One day, we started a meeting together and unexpectedly this person told me that they liked working with me because it was always enjoyable, and that I always managed to find the fun in a situation or piece of work.

Not only was this wonderful to hear, but I was proud that someone else appreciated the joy of finding the light-hearted side of what we do for 40 hours a week. Personally I'm not sure I would like work half as much if I had to be serious all the time – but luckily I've rarely had to be!

What sort of feedback have you received about who you are –
at work or in life?

How has that made you feel?

Does the impression you make on others correspond with the
values that are important to you, and is it the impression you'd
like to make?

8 AUTONOMY AND FEELING IN CONTROL

"I definitely had to tell myself to stay calm, I had to remind myself that the lines are the same lines, the courts are the same size and after every point I told myself 'stay calm'."

COCO GAUFF

(after beating Venus Williams at Wimbledon, aged 15.)

"Doubt is such a strange thing. There'll be times where you succeed and there are times that you fail. So wasting your time doubting whether you're going to be successful or not is pointless. You just put one foot in front of the other, you control what you can control, and then you see what the outcome is."

KOBE BRYANT

My observation is that the feelings of freedom, autonomy and being in control – of oneself, of a situation, of an outcome – are more relevant for some people than others. Some of us find it hard to operate when we are feeling out of control, so reminding ourselves of what we do have autonomy - or agency – over can be extremely helpful.

Having a sense of autonomy can be tremendously empowering and motivational in work and life. And in some circumstances, for some people, regaining a sense of control that has been lost is the first step in moving on.

Choosing your response to events - not always easy but often worth it if you can

Three times the role I've been in has been made redundant. The first time was in my first job after university, when an office move and slight organisational change meant my job didn't exist anymore.

Then twice, within 6 months, in my late 30s, with different companies, when firstly financial pressures and secondly another strategic change, meant that each time my role was not needed.

Every circumstance is different, but redundancy brings multiple challenges to the affected person. This includes uncertainty and financial concerns (even with redundancy pay).

But I think the biggest challenge is often the feeling that someone else is in control of your life, even if only for a brief period of time, and not you. I believe that absolutely the person or people making the redundancy decision are having a significant impact on your life at that moment but they don't control your life. You do that. You decide how to respond and what to focus on in both the short and longer term.

And that knowledge and learning – that you are in charge of you - is then helpful whatever happens to you, redundancy or otherwise.

One of the trickiest things about understanding what is within your control and being able to choose your response is to realise how hard it is in the heat of the moment. Our stress responses are conditioned by our days as cavemen; we tend to revert to fight or flight (although freeze and fawn are now understood to be additional responses to high-stress situations). So taking that step back, getting some perspective and thinking about what you can control isn't always possible in the first reactive moment.

What does make it easier is practice. Getting used to thinking about how you respond to situations and recognising your stress responses and how they play out for you, can help you recognise them earlier. Once you're able to recognise those responses, you can start to be a bit more proactive about choosing when to use them. And just that choice in itself will help you feel more in control of a challenge or stressful situation.

> When have you been able to find a way of stepping back and choosing your response in a stressful situation?
>
> What helped you to take that choice?
>
> How would you use that experience in a future challenge?

Act or be acted upon

Stephen Covey tells a great story in his 7 Habits book under Habit 1 – Be Proactive.

He talks about working with a group of people in the home improvement industry during a heavy recession. When he met them they were down and discouraged.

He writes: "On day 1 the group asked themselves "What is happening to us?" and by the end of the day everyone was even more discouraged."

"On the second day they asked themselves "What's going to happen in the future?" and by the end of that day everyone was even more depressed. Things were going to get worse before they got better, and everyone knew it."

So on the third day they focused on the proactive question. "What is our response? What are we going to do? How can we exercise initiative in this situation?"

Covey describes how a new spirit of excitement, hope, and

proactive awareness concluded the meetings.

Whatever your circumstances, being proactive is often a good step (even proactively deciding to do nothing, for the moment).

I grew up with cats in the house, and being an animal lover, always wanted my own when I had left home. After many years of renting, I'd hoped that my first home would allow for a cat. Unfortunately, the space was limited and without a garden, I didn't feel that there was enough space for a cat.

After a few years of living there, I was going through a tough time. One day, I amazed the friendly colleagues who had been doing their best to cheer me up when I arrived at a meeting smiling, and announced that I had decided to get a cat. I was going to manage the issues inherent in a small house, and the prospect of getting a cat had given me hope that I could get through this tough patch and had something positive to focus on.

As it turned out, I didn't end up getting cats until 18 months later when I moved to a bigger house with a garden. But finding a positive focal point and an action I could take to improve my life helped me get through that tough time.

> When have you found changing your attitude, or focusing on something positive that you could do, has helped you manage a difficult situation?
>
> Why did it make such a difference?

Micro-management is not micro-management if it's agreed

I once managed a boys' football team. One day I said to the boys – they were about 10 or 11 – "I've noticed that you often stop concentrating or stop running during games. Would it help during a game if I keep shouting at you to look around and keep working hard?"

They quite quickly said yes, it would help.

So I spent much of the next match shouting instructions. "John, look around you". "Charlie, keep going". I was really quite shouty.

At the end of the game the manager and a number of parents of the other team came up and told me how outrageous my shouty behaviour was. I thanked them for their feedback but otherwise ignored it.

I wonder if some of them had experienced micro-managing at work. If you are being told what to do all the time – particularly if you already feel capable – it can make you feel frustrated, make you feel incompetent and can affect your motivation, negatively. Many of us have felt this from time to time.

But if you are learning it can be helpful, especially if it has been explained and agreed in advance.

Giving clear, regular, specific instructions can obviously be very helpful in certain circumstances. What felt most important with the boys was that we had talked about it and agreed it beforehand.

When you manage a group or team of people, it's not always straightforward to find out what they need from you as a manager. Sometimes – like the boys Jim coached – their levels of experience and expertise are similar, and you can treat them all the same. Of course, it helps to offer them choices in approach and see what would help them most – as Jim did here.

At other times you may need to lead a group with very diverse levels of experience and skillsets. It can take time to work out how to tailor your approach to what each team member needs as well as what your experience and skillset allows you to offer. Sometimes what is needed is obvious, and sometimes you have to ask. In all cases, trusting your team to know what they need and letting them choose how you work together helps you find a route to success much faster than just imposing on them.

How have you had to tailor your leadership style to what your team needed?

What helped you find ways to shape your style, and what made it harder?

How have you responded if you've been managed in a way that didn't meet your needs?

Three alternative strategies to respond to imposed changes and challenges

I once worked with a group of aspiring employees on a programme to help them prepare for their next role.

In one session we talked about times of change or challenge, or even more generally, and how to maintain motivation by protecting a sense of autonomy. Watching out for sources of frustration, annoyance and energy draining environmental factors, we discussed a strategy of focusing on the things that you can influence – in other words a strategy of 'controlling the controllables'.

In a follow up 1-1 with one of them, Thomas, he taught me an acronym he had made up after the group session called AIM.

It stands for

- Accept
- Influence
- Moan

And he told me he applied this to himself and talked about it to the team of managers he led.

He said with any change happening in the business, or any procedure or situation, you can accept it, influence it or moan about it. And he put it to his team that moaning was an option, but one that probably wouldn't do any good.

I like AIM. It works as an acronym, I can remember it, and the three elements make up a great set of choices.

One of the things I've learned in life is that being heard and having your experience validated is important. Sometimes it can be hard to differentiate having a moan and talking about your experience to understand it better and be able to come to terms with it – which enables you to start accepting it.

It's a really useful question to ask yourself if you feel concerned that you're having a moan. If you haven't talked about something to anyone, and you find it spilling out, your experience probably needs some airtime in order to allow you to gain perspective. If you are able to find ways to accept the situation or the change after being heard, you probably weren't whinging. If you keep on ploughing the same furrow with your complaint, and everyone around you is sick of it – well, either you're complaining, or the problem is so complex that it's going to take a lot of airing!

It's tricky to find the balance and understand when you are just complaining, and when you're using someone else as a sounding board to move forward with your own understanding of a situation.

Have you ever found yourself checking your tendency to moan after talking to someone for a while?

Did that enable you to switch focus from complaining to finding ways to accept or influence the situation?

How did the person listening to you respond?

Confidence from knowing what you are capable of and can control

One of my favourite stories about a sense of mastery and control comes from the great Australian swimmer Ian Thorpe. Back in 2000, ahead of his home Olympics in Sydney, Thorpe was interviewed on the radio and asked if he was going to win 7 gold medals in the pool (he was entered in a total of 7 individual events and relays, and 7 gold medals was certainly a possibility).

On the face of it, that's a lot of pressure. So many little things could go wrong.

In answering the question, Thorpe replied that he knew the training he had done, he knew the shape he was in and he knew the performances that he intended to put in. However he hadn't put that into practice in an Olympic Games yet and he didn't know what other people were capable of doing, so he had no idea how many medals he would get.

Once you've set your goal, and done your prep, you just need to focus on the process and not be drawn - by yourself or others - into getting too far ahead of yourself.

If you can do that you are probably on a good course and it's also a good way of dealing with the pressure of delivering in the moment.

As someone who managed a team of 12 for several years, I got used to holding interviews when team members decided to move onwards and upwards. We would hold fairly intense interviews with a big script of questions designed to both uncover the candidate's technical knowledge as well as getting to understand their personality and how they might fit into a fast-paced work environment. We asked some really tricky questions; "What would your worst enemy say about you?" often stumped candidates.

The one question we never asked was "Where do you see yourself in five years?", simply because it wasn't helpful. The answer you would most likely get would be "Working here..." and even if that wasn't the response, there isn't much else you could say at interview that would honestly answer the question. It certainly wouldn't reveal anything about a candidate's technical skills or how well they'd fit into the team, and we ultimately were recruiting someone to do a job now. Of course, we would focus on developing them appropriately over time but trying to look five years down the line was just getting too far ahead of the immediate need and context.

> When have you found yourself getting ahead of what is needed right now?
>
> What has helped you get things in perspective again?

Dealing with adversity using the Stockdale Paradox (by Kim)

"You must never confuse faith that you will prevail in the end — which you can never afford to lose — with the discipline to confront the most brutal facts of your current reality, whatever they might be."

James Stockdale was a US Navy pilot captured and tortured for 7 years during the Vietnam war. His explanation of how he was able to endure his horrific circumstances has become infamous: he never gave up hope that he would make it home, whilst accepting the conditions he had to endure were awful.

Some of his fellow prisoners remained positive at first but pinned their hopes on being home by Christmas or by the next year. When these milestones passed without change, they lost all hope and succumbed to the torture, never making it home.

Often when someone is facing a challenging situation they are encouraged by others to stay positive, or to keep their chin up. Sometimes this can help someone get through a challenge, but when a really difficult life experience is prolonged and the future seems uncertain, being told to be positive can feel like a kick in the teeth. Trying to be positive and not managing to do so in difficult moments can pile on guilt and the need to try and hide the challenges of the situation from others, all in the name of 'staying positive'!

Following Stockdale's advice and being pragmatic can be really helpful. Accepting that the present situation is incredibly challenging when there is no end in sight makes it possible to hold onto hope that the future will be better, even if it is impossible to imagine right now. That hope for the future is important, but being able to admit that things are tough right now and finding coping strategies is much healthier than trying to hide everything behind a strained smile.

When have you experienced a situation in which being pragmatic was more helpful than being positive? How did that help you have faith that things would get better eventually?

Whilst, thankfully, only the smallest fraction of us will ever have to endure the worst of being a prisoner of war, Kim's interpretation of the Stockdale paradox and how it "makes it possible to hold onto hope that the future will be better", is relevant for many.

By its nature, performance coaching often encourages or demands that people discuss their challenges. I remember coaching a single mum, working full time, during very difficult circumstances in lockdown. It was tough. She had worked extremely hard to get to where she had got to – studying, getting qualifications and putting herself forward.

She told me about how her Mum would say "failure is not an option". This saying had been incredibly useful for her but also – as it turned out - a bit of a millstone around her neck. She acknowledged that her life was hard but there was a never a thought that she might do something like go part time or reduce her levels of responsibility. I heard sometime later that in consultation with her manager and HR she did take a bit of an enforced break.

Somehow the Stockdale paradox can enable you to openly acknowledge that the current demand you are facing is more than you can cope with, without saying that you can't come through it and eventually advance.

Not for the first time in writing this book, this is valuable learning for me.

Staying mindful of the second arrow (also by Kim)

One of the Buddhist stories I find most valuable is the parable of the Two Arrows. The Buddha asks a student:

"If a person is struck by an arrow, is it painful?

If the person is then struck by a second arrow, is it even more painful?"

He then went on to explain,

"In life, we can't always control the first arrow.

However, the second arrow is our reaction to the first. This second arrow is optional."

The second arrow can apply to so many situations; beating yourself up or being self-critical about a mistake. Catastrophising about what could go wrong. Feeling guilty or imperfect. Those 3am moments where your brain replays everything you have ever done wrong in your life. Even l'espirit d'escalier (staircase thoughts) – i.e., the perfect response to a question or challenge coming hours too late.

I don't think anyone can escape the second arrow, or sometimes even the third or fourth arrow either! The wisdom here is in learning to recognise the extra arrows, and let them go. As ever, it is easier with practice to look at your response to a situation and choose to just let the first arrow be.

When have you found yourself able to let go of the second arrow?

How did that make you feel, and did it help you?

I love Kim's second arrow story, having just read it for the first time. That Buddha was pretty wise.

Bob Rotella tells a story about a basketball player missing a free throw (where, after a foul by the other team, you get to take your shot in your own time, without the opposition defending you). On this occasion the player, the best free throw shooter in the team, not only missed the throw but the ball fell so short it didn't even make contact with the ring. An 'air shot'.

Sometime later the player was talking to Rotella, a sports psychologist, because his percentage success rate in taking free throws had gone down. It turned out that he had been so mortified at throwing an air shot that he had resolved to never throw another and feel the same pain again. As a result he was now fractionally overthrowing the ball each time, and as a result was missing fractionally more.

I suspect that beating yourself up is a defence mechanism – a form of flight or freezing – that we do to protect ourselves from making the same mistake again. Whilst I can't remember specific examples, I can remember using the basketball free throw shooter story in my coaching work.

The second arrow story tells the principle really well.

Moves and Moving On from Others' Decisions

Sometimes people make decisions that affect us, which we just can't fathom. At some point, even though it might puzzle us, bug us or bother us, we eventually move on and trough.

A few years ago our neighbour was away and, together with a couple of other neighbours, we were keeping an eye on her house. She had arranged for a builder she knew, who she had used many times before, to come and do a few jobs while the house was empty. When he arrived one of the things he first noticed were some strange marks on the front door, which he was suspicious might have been caused by someone trying to break in.

We were a bit shocked. The terraced houses open right onto the street with the smallest of front gardens and we were taken aback that someone might have the audacity to try and break in in broad view of everyone. Of course we started to ask questions. Did they know the neighbour was away? Had they been staking the house out, and who next? Would they come back and try again?

We decided not to disturb the neighbour on her holiday but did contact the local police who sent someone round to have a look. One helpful bit of advice we received was "don't bother to try and work out the mind of a petty criminal. It could have been planned but was as likely to be opportunistic. It could have been by a serial burglar or a one-off by someone passing by". It was good advice. Don't waste your time guessing.

This is true for us when managers or senior leaders make decisions that make no sense to us or even seem - from our perspective - to make things worse. A company I once worked for moved some of their head office functions from the north-west, where they own the land and buildings, to the south-east where they rented expensive premises on a business park. Mass disruption, people moved, people left, and we weren't even in London, with a presence there, but just inside the M25 near Watford. I eventually accepted that no-one was going to be able to provide me with the rationale for the move which would satisfy me. Move on, Jim.

The best bit about my neighbour story is that when she got home a week or two later, she said "Oh, those marks, they've been there for years!"

Like Jim, I once worked for an organisation that made a major office move. Unlike Jim's move, it made business sense - moving from a slightly tired grand old country house which could be sold for a significant sum to developers, investing the proceeds, and renting a smaller office area in a modern town-centre building. Moving from lots of small offices holding a few people in a maze-like setup to having an open-plan area was logical- people could collaborate more easily and no-one was hidden away from the rest of the organisation.

What was similar to Jim's office move was that this change was also deeply unpopular with staff. Ways of working and settled routines were upended overnight, and people felt very uncomfortable and as if they were under Big Brother-esque surveillance in the open-plan area. Losing subsidised lunches and a lovely garden didn't help! Lots of people left and there was a lot of grumbling discontent and wanting to go back to the old ways of working.

Despite understanding the business rationale for the decision, it wasn't an easy transition for anyone. Eventually I too left, primarily because the move meant that my job had changed, and it was time to move on.

What both stories show us is that whether you understand a decision and the consequent changes or not, if things are difficult you eventually have to find a way to move on. Whether that is Jim accepting that he wouldn't get the answers he sought, or me deciding that I needed a new job, a conscious decision to get past a difficult situation is often a necessity for progress.

When have you had to make a conscious decision to 'move on' from something that is challenging you?

What helped you move on, and what would you say to someone else in the same boat?

9 DEVELOPMENT

"You cannot teach a man anything; you can only help him to find it within himself."

GALILEO

"I don't want to be an expert; I want to be a student."

RAY MEARS, DESERT ISLAND DISCS

"You can only think and feel from that part in our development"

JOHN BUTLER

The majority of my working life has been in the area of development. Development feels important to me – like I would get itchy feet if I didn't feel I were continuing to grow in some way or direction. I remember the thought stopping feeling I had during the conversation described in the first story below.

One of my own discoveries has been how failure and mistakes are often accompanied by learning. It's as if the growth that can occur is somehow compensation for the pain and disappointment. I love Katherine Grainger's thoughts in the story in this section that mentions her.

Who has responsibility for your development, and keeping it with you!

I was once out in Scotland with a sales consultant, Michael, who worked for the same business as me (Guardian Financial Services, part of GRE). We were talking to the customer about the development of staff in the customer's business – because we had training resources we could potentially put into the customer's business, as part of a negotiation, in order to get some sort of return.

During the conversation my colleague, Michael, proudly told the customer that "where we work we've been given responsibility for our own development".

As someone who had always, largely, felt responsible for his own development, I found Michael's comment really odd. Briefly I was no longer tuned in to what was being said as my thoughts headed elsewhere. I had questions. As the conversation continued I found myself asking myself "who had Michael given responsibility to, when had Michael given it away in the first place, and when was it returned?"

I know that managers in organisations sometimes have training budgets or influence over things like internal courses or study leave, but for the most part, I think we have responsibility for our own development.

Being, keeping, staying responsible for your own development means no one else but you can neglect it. Give it away to others only after some consideration. And don't neglect it.

Back in my rugby-playing days, I took my part in the team very seriously.

Although it was an uphill struggle because I am naturally uncoordinated, didn't build muscle easily, and I was never particularly fit, I committed to being the best I could be. I attended every training session, went out running (admittedly only a few miles) in my own time, and during the summers met up with a friend in the park to work through press-ups and sprints. My teammates did the same, to the extent they could around what were often incredibly demanding jobs working shifts or in the City.

At the start of one season, we had a new volunteer coach take over and he didn't fit in particularly well with the team ethos. One evening he announced that we would have a 'review' session in the bar instead of our usual training the following week. I put my hand up and asked whether there would be any physical work involved, as if not I would go for a run beforehand to ensure my fitness levels didn't drop too much. He was entirely perplexed and didn't seem to understand why I would voluntarily go for a run instead of enjoying a night off in a nice warm room.

He didn't stay with the team for much longer.

Have you ever had to explain your commitment to your own development to someone who didn't understand it?

How would you explain what drives your desire to improve?

Is there anyone that you would share responsibility for your development with – like a coach or a manager?

Sharpen the Saw

A boss in my mid-thirties was a chap called Mike Gummerson. One Christmas he gave each of the team a book and he bought me Stephen Covey's 7 Habits book.

I don't know why Mike decided to give me that book then, but I'm glad he did. I would have been in my mid-thirties and was keen to read, learn and grow.

Sharpen the Saw is Stephen Covey's 7th Habit. I've come across this story – or attitude – described in different ways.

Covey's story goes like this:

> *Suppose you were to come upon someone in the woods working feverishly to saw down a tree.*
>
> *"What are you doing?" you ask.*
>
> *"Can't you see?" comes the impatient reply. "I'm sawing down this tree."*
>
> *"You look exhausted!" you exclaim. "How long have you been at it?"*
>
> *"Over five hours," he returns, "and I'm beat! This is hard work."*
>
> *"Well, why don't you take a break for a few minutes and sharpen that saw?" you inquire. "I'm sure it would go a lot faster."*
>
> *"I don't have time to sharpen the saw," the man says empathetically. "I'm too busy sawing!"*

It links closely to the Learning Cycle: Plan – Do – Review – Conclude (often abbreviated, because it's snappier, to Plan, Do, Review).

The learning cycle got introduced to me in my first ever training job, but I now see it as a high performance cycle. Plan, Do, Review. For many people, their roles and all the tasks they have to do, mean they are never finished. They never run out of work.

So for them, especially when they are very busy, the reviewing part gets squeezed or frequently doesn't happen. When they're really, really busy planning gets impacted too and they end up in an ongoing cycle of just doing. Which is great because they get a lot done but not so good if they want to get better.

In that scenario, pausing, reviewing and sharpening the saw has to become a conscious effort.

I once read some really great advice that a colleague shared in an internal blog. They explained that you will never finish your work to-do list, and accepting that fact will allow you to manage both your work and your work-life balance with a little more freedom and perspective.

Reading that felt like a big relief, almost permission to not finish the list of work to do, and that not doing so would be ok. I often get caught up in trying to finish something in order to tick it off the list, and I have had to learn to take that metaphorical step back, ask myself if I will be able to finish it in the time I wanted to, and what the price of doing so will be – whether that is not having any downtime, or getting to bed late, or missing a meeting.

When I'm working at home, it can be easy to be sucked into busy-ness and feeling I need to finish a set number of things before I can stop work for the evening or weekend – even if that means I'm still typing away at 8.30pm on a Friday night.

Being able to stop and sharpen the Saw means I can take a break and likely do a better job the following week instead of pushing on out of stubbornness.

What helps you step back and take stock when you are busy?

How does that help you succeed?

Helping potential to come out from within

An Italian chap, Michael, told a great story in a session I was running for managers looking to develop their performance coaching capabilities.

We were talking about the role, and the challenge, of the leader/manager in developing others. Many leaders and managers are working with team members who have obvious or perhaps hidden potential. Part of the challenge is to provide the environment and support to allow as much of that potential to be fulfilled as possible.

Michael was in a small group of three that I joined. He was explaining that Michelangelo used to say, before starting a sculpture, that the sculpture already exists in the rock. All he had to do, carefully and skilfully with his tools, was remove the unneeded bits of rock to reveal the form underneath.

There's a definition of performance that says Performance = Potential minus Interference and this story reminds me of that definition, with a coach or manager playing a role to help remove the interference.

There are many instances of interference - lack of opportunity, other people somehow in the way, too much focus on the short term or people getting in their own way with unhelpful thinking.

The leader/manager is often in a position to help individuals to get closer to fulfilling their potential and being all they can be. They do this through all the usual ways - feedback, coaching, providing opportunities (a big one), supporting and encouraging.

I once managed a team where my role was to be the manager. Although I understood the work that they did, I hadn't done their roles myself nor built up the years of experience that made them high performers. As someone who believes that you shouldn't ask others to do things that you're not willing to do yourself, it was hard for me to ask them to dig deep at busy times knowing that if I tried to take some of the burden myself, I'd likely slow things down rather than helping.

One day, during a light-hearted conversation across the desks, I pulled some jargon together into an impressive sounding sentence. My team seemed surprised that I could come up with something like that off the cuff, and one of them pointed out that this was why I went to meetings with the rest of the organisation and they didn't. It reminded me that my skills and experience were best placed to help them by doing the work that they weren't familiar with and enabled them to do their jobs, whether that was liaising with suppliers or the rest of the organisation, or any number of other things. This understanding of my role as different really helped me become comfortable with leading the team without being able to put my shoulder to the wheel in the same way.

> When you have led or managed others, how did you find the right ways to enable them to succeed and flourish?
>
> How often did you need to change your approach – whether from steering to pushing, or from running ahead and clearing the way to offering much-needed support?

If there is a particular job or career you want or you want to be something in particular

Sometime when I had been in a training role for a few years and was starting to do some internal consultancy work I received some excellent careers advice. At the time the company I was in, or perhaps in the industry at the time, there was an increased interest in coaching.

I was very interested. But I felt unqualified or at least inexperienced as a coach. I wasn't a manager and didn't have direct reports to coach. But nevertheless I was really interested in coaching.

Then someone told me "if you want to be a coach start coaching people". And so I did. I asked people I was training if they were interested in a coaching conversation. When talking to people I started asking them more questions about what they were trying to achieve or what they were considering doing, and I booked myself on an excellent 1-day coaching conference run by the CIPD.

All this served me very well, but the advice acted as a catalyst. Maybe I was lucky to have the opportunity to explore my interest, and practise. I feel grateful for the opportunity, but it still needed taking.

If you want to be a "blank" start "blanking".

It can be easy to talk ourselves out of things we want to do.

- *'That new job looks great but it pays so much more than I earn right now so I'd probably never get it, plus I hate doing applications.'*

- *'Well, of course I can do something about this problem, but as it's part of a wider systemic issue that will take years to fix, is it really worth it?'*

It doesn't take much to convince ourselves. Sometimes, the best way to decide to take the plunge is to ask yourself how you'd feel if someone else took that opportunity? If you would feel jealous, then perhaps it's time to push yourself to take that shot.
The other excellent advice I've been given in scenarios like this is that Perfect is the enemy of good or sometimes even Perfect is the enemy of done.

In most cases, waiting for the perfect moment – such as someone knocking on your door and whisking you off to coaching school free of charge (!) – prevents you from ever finishing (or even starting) something that could be very good as is, without delaying it to seek perfection.

What holds you back from doing what you want to do?

How do you talk yourself out of making a change or starting something new?

Where are you when you do your best thinking?

I once ran a joint training session with about 50 people, with a lovely chap called Rob, then in a training role at Virgin Media. It was the first time we had worked together, and one of the benefits of working with someone new is that you often learn new things.

Rob had the task of opening the session up and setting the tone for what was to come.

He asked everyone to take a blank piece of A4 paper from the centre of the table in front of them. He then asked them to think of where they are when they do their best thinking. Then he asked them to draw a picture of themself, doing what they are doing, when they're doing their best thinking. He explained that it wasn't a drawing competition!

Then he asked them to write their name on their paper, to screw it into a ball, and to throw it to him.

As the balls of paper came flying in Rob started opening a few and asking the people to talk about their drawing and what they were doing. After 4 or 5 a few things began to become obvious:

No-one was at their desk
Many people were doing mindless tasks
A few involved either being stationary or physical movement of some sort

It was a great exercise of Rob's.

To me, if you're in a role that requires you to do good thinking, this means finding and creating the space to do that. If you don't do it consciously you risk it not happening.

And that space could be anywhere that works for you - and it's quite likely that it's not at your desk or even 'at work'.

I have been lucky enough to experience this exercise for myself; and like Jim says, the room was full of answers like commuting, walking the dog, in the shower. I remember wanting more time as I wanted to draw a lot of pictures to represent all the places where I'd had great ideas. There are even social media accounts and pages dedicated to shower thoughts, so finding mental clarity there is clearly a common occurrence for many people!

Often I find myself wandering away from my desk to say hallo to the cat, or out into the garden in the summer. Having a moment to pause and do something that allows my brain a bit of perspective and reflection time makes a big difference to both the quality of my ideas, but also my ability to work effectively. I still have my best ideas in the shower though!

Where do you have your best ideas?

How could you give yourself more opportunities to do your best thinking?

Learning from successes and from failures

I've never read world cup winning rugby coach Sir Clive Woodward's books but I've heard that he talks about a change he made when taking over England as team manager.

Apparently at the time victories were celebrated with beers and cheers and defeats were pored over to work out what went wrong. As I understand it he made the focus much more about understanding what went right, in winning.

It feels to me that both approaches can be very useful. Celebrate success and seek to learn from it too. In defeat celebrate the effort, that you were there - "actually in the arena" - that you tried, and seek to learn from the defeat too.

With my professional hat on, as a Knowledge Manager the discipline often focuses on lessons learned – interrogating a situation that has gone wrong or a project that has run into difficulty to find out why. It's important for organisations to be able to talk about things going wrong and find out why they failed in an open manner – not to blame anyone, but in order to understand the problems and either fix them or provide ways to mitigate them in future. This can be challenging, as often these reviews capture what has gone wrong by making a note of it but don't result in action to fix or prevent the problems.

However, this focus – while important – can also mean that we don't interrogate success in the same way. After all, things going right can be just as much down to small things as a project that runs into trouble.
Whether it is the culture of the organisation allowing (or preventing) collaboration, the expertise of the individuals involved, the way that the project or task was approached and at times, something as seemingly unimportant as the weather, small and often taken-for-granted contextual factors can play a big part.

Understanding them, whether the work succeeds or fails, is one of the biggest opportunities there is for building on them to create future excellence.

> How do you reflect on successes and challenges?
>
> Do you talk about them and why things went the way they did? Or is it something you'd like to do more of?
>
> Which questions help you understand what has happened?

The rich value in learning from defeat

Annie Vernon's book Mind Games is a great read. Part autobiographical – she was an Olympic medal winning rower - it features lots of interviews and stories from other top athletes, from top coaches and from sports psychologists. While it's not an academic read, it is a lot more than just anecdotes.

She mentions and quotes her ex-team mate Katherine Grainger a number of times. One of the things I remember well is where Katherine Grainger is talking about successes and defeats. She says that whilst successes are sweet, defeats last much longer, and ultimately are the things you learn from most.

Here's the full extract I'm referring to. I've shared it with people many times:

"Olympic rower Katherine Grainger admits: Defeats last longer, at some emotional level. What I've always found is that I enjoy and move on quite quickly from success. Defeat stays with me, I linger over [it], and it's the thing that will wake me up at five in the morning and I won't go back to sleep because it annoys me, because it makes me think in some way we must have got something wrong

– and defeats will linger in that way. They last longer and are hence a lower low than the highest of high. But I also think with a bit of distance you also appreciate them, because they are inevitably the biggest learning experience. The low points and the disappointing ones will be the most effective learning you'll ever have, as an athlete and also as a person."

When I first learnt to play rugby, I was out in New Zealand on my gap year. Someone else in the same hostel I was staying long-term in tipped me off that the village club were trying to restart their women's team, and as the pitch was about two minutes away
I decided to give it a go. I was incredibly green and not co-ordinated, but I was determined to improve.
We managed to pull a team together and competed in the 6-team local league.
For some reason we played on Wednesday evenings with two double-headers at a large sports ground in the area, and the third match would be played an hour's drive away where one out-of-area team would meet their opponents halfway.

To be honest, we were pretty terrible. We were playing against established teams with seriously good players and we were a pretty ragtag bunch of green newbies and a couple of good individuals. We were being regularly beaten by scores of over a hundred points, although the rural team was being downed by scores closer to two hundred. I certainly didn't have a clue what I was doing and was regularly offside or in the way – luckily the refs clearly appreciated I was clueless! We did our best to grow together as a group, but it was hard as socialising after the game was tricky midweek. We targeted the game against the rural team as our goal for the season; and we did win it. The minibus journey back home was jubilant!

Ultimately, we didn't learn as much about our game from the defeats as maybe we should have done – we expected to lose a lot of the games because we were just outclassed.
What our coaches did do incredibly well was keep us motivated in the face of trouncing after trouncing. Because they didn't expect us to win, they

focused on what we did do well, and praised our improvement. I still remember – more than twenty years on – the joking in the bar that I would return to England and steamroller everyone having learned rugby the hard way.

They even reckoned I would be called 'the English Express" once I had found my feet (instead of standing on other people's!) as I would be as unstoppable as a speeding train…. I might not have been very good but knowing that the coaches saw potential in me probably kept me in the game.

Learning from defeat isn't the same as learning how to win – but sometimes that doesn't matter as much as what you take from it. Although winning can be important too!

> What have you learned from defeat?
>
> Has it helped you improve and win in future, or has it helped you in other ways?

Giving feedback is a skill

Appropriate feedback, delivered well, will improve confidence. Even if initially, on the face of it, it's negative, it can help people to know what to do differently in the future.

I was once on a presentation skills course where we took it in turns to present. The presenter would then leave the room while the rest of the half a dozen people would agree what feedback they wanted to give. A rota determined who would give the feedback using a strict methodology of 1. Something good to start with 2. Something to work on and 3. Something good to finish with (I think the thinking is that the two good things will outweigh the 'bad' thing on the confidence scales).

One presentation was really bad. In our huddle we struggled to find anything good to say at all to the presenter. With time running out before they returned, we looked helplessly at the person whose turn it was to be giving the feedback.

The presenter came back in and sat down and person said, "Nice tie, crap presentation, but nice tie".

I don't think that was the best way. Feedback is often best if it's given some thought, like a gift.

That 'feedback is a gift' metaphor can be a bit trite, but in some ways it's true. The gift is the new knowledge and self-awareness you have - maybe how you made someone feel.

The analogy of giving and receiving an actual gift works well too. As the giver:

- Make the gift personal if you can
- Wrap it well
- Think about when to give it
- Think about where to give it
- Think about how to give it

As the receiver, whether you love it, hate it or are indifferent to it, first of all say "thank you" (then you can treasure it, put it one side, put it in the loft or take it to a car boot sale).

Feedback is a tricky one. We all want to receive it, both to understand how we are performing, and to know how to improve.
Of course, it would be better if it was always positive, but that's not realistic. And naturally, it can be hard to give feedback if you think that it won't be well-received.
After all, giving someone platitudes and telling them what you think they want to hear, rather than having a difficult conversation, often feels much safer and less stressful than finding the right words and moment to tell

them something you feel is negative.

Of course, what is far worse than negative feedback is no feedback – or feedback that you don't believe is sincere. If you're pretty certain that someone giving you feedback has no idea about what you do or hasn't paid any attention to the work they're responding to, you won't take that feedback seriously at all. If you don't get any feedback at all, it can be very dispiriting and isolating.

At the same time, feedback can come in more subtle ways, and sometimes it can be difficult to recognise it if it comes at the wrong time or if (if you're like me) it doesn't come packaged as feedback.

How can you recognise informal feedback more easily?

What is the best way to seek out feedback if you feel you're not receiving it – either at all or with genuine intent?

And how can you use your experiences of difficult or insincere feedback to shape the feedback you give to others?

Never too old to learn – and what you know might be helpful to someone else

They say you're never too old to learn and none of us is ever the finished article.

I coached a 50-something, sport loving CEO who was between jobs and, perhaps unsurprisingly, we got onto the subject of dealing with self-doubt. I started talking about things like our inner voice and the term "self-talk", which he had never heard before.

When I explained the concept of self-talk, it's impact and strategies, he found it really helpful. I was surprised that he'd never heard the term or come across the strategies - because to me the subject was familiar and everyday. That will teach me to assume that just because someone is in their 50s, and professionally successful, they know everything!

It also makes me wonder what things others know, that I've never heard of, that I would find incredibly useful.

When I was a fairly small child, say 6 or 7, I was looking through a book at school about reptiles.

My parents and grandparents had all been born in South Africa and had an interest in wildlife (my Uncle was once chased by a rhino whilst doing research in the Kruger National Park).

I came home from school excited to tell them about a crocodile I had learned about in this book, that had a long thin snout.

The book hadn't said anything more about gharials aside from providing the name and a picture of the head and jaws, so when the adults in the family asked for more details – where was it from, how big was it – I couldn't answer.

They didn't seem convinced and it wasn't listed in their dictionary or any of their books when we looked for it. I was left with impression that everyone rather thought this was a figment of my imagination or a mythical creature.

Years later, I was reading the newspaper at my grandparents' house – they read The Times daily – and it featured an article about gharials with a picture, probably related to conservation efforts. I was finally able to prove that they existed!

Whilst it would be much easier nowadays to prove the existence of an animal my family had never heard of; I've always been a little perplexed that well-educated and intellectually curious adult assumed that I couldn't possibly have stumbled upon something they didn't know about.

> When have you been surprised to discover something that you didn't know about before? And how receptive were you to learning something new?

Learning and change often (always?) come from a change of thinking

The sound of learning is a beautiful sound, but it's not always so easy to hear.

I was sitting at the kitchen table one time, finishing a Christmas puzzle – or at least trying to (they can be slow going, especially towards the end when you've done all the easier bits) – and in the room next door my partner Rachel was maths tutoring, online.

She was explaining and asking questions, but her pupil was struggling. Rachel was prompting but trying not to simply give the answers away without the element of discovery and learning. My ear got really tuned in to the conversation and to the young male, teenage voice at the other end of a Zoom call.

Then, after silences and stutters, I heard him excitedly say, "no, wait!". He knew he knew the answer, but he didn't have it yet, but he knew it was there, in his grasp. He didn't want Rachel to say it, or even help. It just needed a couple more cogs to turn and he had cracked it! Eureka!

"No, wait" was the sound of learning happening.

Sometimes as a coach the learning comes in the pauses.

Some of my best coaching – when the other person has had a 'light bulb' moment – has happened when I'm thinking 'it's my turn to say something. I need to respond or ask another question', but I'm not sure precisely what to say next.

And in that silence, that golden silence, that precious thinking time, the other person has a thought or an idea, that is their best solution or next step. It's the sound of learning! Bingo!!

I love it.

Being able to leave a pause in conversation is definitely an acquired skill. It's always easier to tell someone the answer rather than prompt them in the right way to reach it themselves. And it's definitely easier if you're not comfortable with the person you're talking to and want to maintain control of the conversation

How do you find ways to help yourself let pauses happen, and to let the people you are talking to find answers themselves?

How do you feel when they do have a Eureka moment, and can take ownership of their own leap forward?

10 BEING ALL YOU CAN BE (BEING YOUR BEST)

"What lies behind us, and what lies ahead of us, pales into insignificance compared with what lies within us."

EMMERSON

"He was always practising; I wish I'd done the same."

JIMMY WHITE ON STEPHEN HENDRY

'Performing at your best', 'fulfilling your potential', 'being a high performer'. These are all everyday phrases and things that many of us aspire to.

'Being the best you can be' is for the most part a helpful mantra. Though it gives lots of scope for defining what that means to you personally in different contexts.

These stories are about these phrases, in some senses, about what they mean and in some ways how to be them.

Being, compared to endlessly striving

Jonny Wilkinson is an interesting person. Not necessarily the most interesting person in the whole world but much more so than average.

As I understand it he has an obsessive personality that caused him to train and practice in his quest for perfection.

When I heard him interviewed on the High Performance podcast in about 2021 he sounded like someone who had reflected deeply. Some of what he said sounded quite eastern, quite Buddhist, in its meaning.

He talked about hearing people say they wanted to "leave a legacy". He seemed to be questioning if this was the latest fad. And he questioned the idea of being the best you can be, or fulfilling your potential. He was asking 'what is that', to fulfil your potential. His thoughts seemed to be that if you 'reached' your potential, what then? Wouldn't there always be a next potential to chase? And he seemed to be questioning the value of chasing, and striving and reaching for something that you could never reach.

He was though definitely advocating learning, and exploring and curiosity. But he said that for him, in any given situation, he was less interested in being the best he could be but more about being all that he can be. I think he meant bringing all of him to the moment, whatever that moment was.

It definitely resonated with me. Lots of reflection and growth, but very selective with striving and stretching.

I often listen to a particular Buddhist teacher's audio recordings; his name is Gil Fronsdal, and he teaches and practices near San Francisco as part of the American Vipassana tradition of Buddhism. He has a lovely serene voice as well as being very wise, and several of his stories have stuck in my mind.

One story in particular often comes to mind when people talk to me about wanting to leave a legacy or do something important. Gil talked one day about his experiences of speaking to people at the end of their lives, who were disappointed that they hadn't achieved something 'big' as a legacy. And his simple reflection was that when he thought about the people who made the biggest difference in the world, it was often those who lived in a way that brought happiness, joy, or peace to those around them.
Having a positive impact on the world around you seemed a much greater

legacy than achieving something 'big'.

> Do you feel driven to achieve something big, or do you prefer to focus on being all you can be, like Jonny Wilkinson?
>
> How could you be your best in any given moment, and what would impact would that have on the people around you?

The fundamental principle of looking after yourself

None of us sets out to be ill, but sometimes people make choices that don't seem like common sense, or don't keep them on a path of wellness. And there's no sense whatsoever in getting ill – because then you can't work as well, or at all.

Spotting the signs that you need to rest, or do something differently, is really useful.

At one point in my late teens I was thinking of applying to be a doctor. My Mum was the theatre sister in the local hospital and she offered me the chance to go and watch them perform their 'list'. I wasn't at all squeamish and thought this was a good idea.

We went in early so she could show me around. I remember her saying quite clearly and firmly, "You will be standing here, (she pointed to a spot on the floor) and for heaven's sake don't faint, as you will be in the way, and no-one will have time to look after you. So if you start to feel light headed go out straight away".

The first operation (in this small local hospital) was to remove a pin from someone's broken leg. A tourniquet was applied to stop the flow/loss of blood and when the surgeon made the first cut with his scalpel a single trickle of bright red blood ran down the unnaturally white limb before me.

Whether it was to do with the blood, the antiseptic smelling mask I was wearing or_something else, I immediately felt woozy, so, remembering Mum's words, I went outside into the corridor and sat down in a chair. Shortly after a porter came by who asked if I was ok. When I explained he helpfully suggested I watched for a while through the window from between the two sets of double doors, and when I was ready I could go back in. Which is exactly what I did.

So "don't fall over". This is good advice, when you can.

Take the steps you need to take before you get to that point – and that might mean listening to others who know, or can foresee, what you don't know or can't see.

We live in a world where we're expected to be 'on' all the time. Screens, emails, texts, working from home, working from your phone; none of these concepts were part of our everyday lives 20 years ago. We've also – in the West – become accustomed to the myth that wellness is a result of eating well, exercising, and doing prescribed activities such as yoga or meditating. Of course, all of those things help us be and stay healthy. But this mindset can also mean that we blame and 'other' people who become unwell.

This has become really stark in the last few years since the start of the Covid pandemic. Initial warnings suggested that you would only be particularly hard hit if you were old. The narrative then changed to 'other' people with underlying conditions, as if anyone who might have something wrong with their health didn't deserve to survive a bout of Covid.

It was far easier to dismiss 'underlying conditions' or find phrases like 'with, not of, Covid' comforting than to confront the reality that minor health conditions such as eczema, or being pregnant, or having a sprained ankle would all be considered underlying conditions. It's actually looking increasingly likely that the biggest risk factors for Covid and Long Covid are genetic, and about how your body forms its own immune response to a rapidly mutating virus.

All of this makes it very hard to then accept not only being unwell or the risk of becoming unwell, but also that stopping and resting can be restorative. We think we can power through illness by carrying on with work, or keeping up with exercise, without listening to our bodies and what they need.

When have you had to really listen to yourself and trust what your body was telling you to do?

How did that help?

Choosing what to worry about or not worry about

Once, years ago, before I knew much about mindset or focus or these things, I remember seeing a news reporter on TV out on the street interviewing people after a big storm.

I remember clearly a brief exchange with a late middle aged, or possibly older, man. During the storm a house chimney had become loose and fallen on top of his car, practically writing it off.

What I really remember, with great clarity, was his complete lack of concern about the situation. He wasn't laughing but wasn't worried either. The reporter was pressing him – as if wanting to hear how upset the man was or how devastated he was by events - but the man simply said he was insured and it would all get sorted.

His composure, rationale and perspective really struck a chord, despite the reporter's efforts to unsettle him or make him seem put out in order to get a story. His acceptance was the story.

He seemed to epitomise the Shakespeare line, first told to me by Michael Brooke, "there's nothing that is good or bad, only thinking makes it so".

Another of my favourite Gil Fronsdal pieces of advice is about worrying. We all worry, and sometimes that can be useful – it's a fairly primeval mechanism we developed as hunter-gatherers to remind us to think about what a sabre-toothed tiger might be up to and where it might hide. Probably.

But if you find yourself worrying about something in an all-consuming way, what happens if you postpone your worrying until tomorrow? After all, if you really need to worry, the worry will be there to come back to. It's ok to take some time off from it.

Sometimes taking that break from a worry can be liberating, and help you regain control over it. Finding that sense of control about a situation can help you choose whether to keep worrying, or whether to take some action to mitigate things. After all, if you can't do anything about the problem, and the worry allows you to take time off, is it really worth coming back to?

What helps you put worrying aside, and what techniques do you use to do so?

The Luck Factor – how to be lucky

The Luck Factor is a great book by Dr Richard Wiseman.

He studied Luck. He was an amateur magician who once, while doing a card trick with a lady volunteer audience member, was intrigued by the strength of her conviction that she was lucky.

He set about a research study and advertised for people to take part who considered themselves as lucky and people who considered themselves unlucky.

He gave everyone some scenarios and put them through some experiences to test them. One was to imagine they were in a bank, queuing to speak to a cashier, at the same time as an armed robbery takes place, in which they get shot in the arm.

He asked them what they thought of that? And of course, all the people who considered themselves lucky said, "How lucky am I?! I could have been killed. Now I have a story to dine out on for years. I'm so lucky".

And all the people who considered themselves unlucky said. "How unlucky am I? Why me? That's typical of my luck to happen to be in the bank on that day. And be the one who actually gets shot. I'm so unlucky".

Wiseman concluded that luck is not 'luck' but down to 4 factors:
- Lucky people expect to be lucky
- Lucky people interpret events in their favour (perpetuating their self-perception)
- Lucky people increase their chances of being lucky (e.g. they buy that raffle ticket)
- Lucky people trust their instincts

And a true story, is that I was part way through reading the book when I went on a work trip to Leeds.

As I drove up the M1 motorway the day before my 9.00am meeting, to stay overnight, I realised to my horror that I had left my suit at home. Luckily I realised a few junctions before the Sheffield turn, and Meadowhall, the huge shopping mall, which was by the motorway. I was able to get off, go to a shop and get a new suit within half an hour. And I needed a new suit anyway. If I'd realised when I got to Leeds the shops would have been shut and I would have been too late.

How lucky am I??

I work for an organisation that had issued all staff with laptops not long before I joined. It was great to have new IT kit that worked really well and could be taken to meetings or used to work from home without any difficulty. A couple of months after I started, there was a major fire at the weekend that destroyed the upper floors and the roof of one half of the office. It was a bit of a shock, but everyone pulled together to respond to the crisis, and within a few days there were rotas allowing people to come in and work in the usable half of the office. A few weeks later we had a rented temporary office half a mile away for staff who didn't need to be in the original location, and everyone was settled into an office routine again.

A few weeks after the new office opened – about six weeks after the fire – the UK went into Covid lockdown and everyone had to work from home. Having been through the sudden changes after the fire, my colleagues were very relaxed about having to make the changes and felt confident in being able to do everything remotely.

A year or so later, I interviewed the departing CEO and asked whether he felt that we had been lucky to have the fire because our response to it meant we had 'battle-tested' everything we needed to put into place when lockdown started.

He simply replied; "We made our own luck."

He felt that the hard work that had been done long before the fire in upgrading our IT and enabling staff to work remotely- which meant that in both situations we were well-placed to handle events.

A friend of mine regularly enters competitions, and even has a huge box of postcards to use for free entry into paid-for contests. She often wins things, and the time she puts in clearly pays off. Her mantra is "You've got to be in it to win it."

Again, she makes her own luck by making sure she has given herself the opportunity to win, to be lucky.

Are you a 'lucky' person?

What would make you feel lucky?

What could you do or change to be 'luckier'?

An example of how extremes of perspective can be helpful

When you are right bang smack in the middle of something that seems really crucial it can feel all-consuming and like the most important thing in the world.

And when you're thinking like that it can affect all sorts of things like your decision making and even your health. And not in a good way! Maintaining perspective can be extremely useful though not always easy to do.

In 2008 Katherine Grainger had just competed in her 3rd Olympics and won her third silver medal. Winning three silvers is a pretty serious achievement but in Beijing her crew had_come within a gnat's whisker of what was proving to be a very elusive and very difficult gold medal. They were beaten by a boat containing the top four Chinese rowers.

Two weeks or so later she was interviewed on BBC Radio Scotland and I was listening. She was asked if she was planning to carry on to what would be her fourth Olympics, in London in 2012, to compete for that special, so far elusive, prize.

She paused, and then described the (phenomenal) commitment that was required in her sport, rowing. Training and competing were extremely challenging. In an Olympic year the build-up was intense and there was hardly a day off. The commitment had to be total and be relentless.

She paused. At the same time, she calmly explained, all she was doing was moving a bit of plastic 2000m across a stretch of water and it was totally meaningless!

She said that to do what she did, you had to maintain these two thoughts at the same time. That what you are doing is the most important thing in the world and meaningless.

Wow!

You had, she said, in weighing up whether to continue or not, to weigh up those two things. Many of us get wrapped up in the importance of what we do or our own importance. With the exception of some exceptional people – doctors, nurses, emergency medical staff etc – most of what most of us do is largely meaningless – or at least its (relative) importance can be very usefully seen in perspective.

Work hard on the things that are important. Work really hard if they're really important. But keep Katherine Grainger's paradoxical thinking in mind. Even what seems the most important thing ever, is in some way meaningless.

When I'm struggling to find perspective, I like to watch a short video on YouTube. You've probably seen it before, or at least would recognise it when you watched it. It's an audio recording of American astronomer Carl Sagan's Pale Blue Dot speech, accompanied by the imagery that inspired it.

The video starts by inviting you to 'Consider that dot…', over a photo with an arrow pointing at a bright pixel in a beam of light.

The photo was taken by Voyager 1, of Earth, from 3.7 billion miles away.

Sagan reminds the listener of the vastness of the universe, and by comparison, the insignificance of our problems and worries. Fortunately he manages to do so in a very inspiring and uplifting manner – he was a well-known science communicator and public figure!

The video never fails to make me feel calmer and in greater control of my sense of perspective. Although my problems are important right now, they will fade into insignificance in a short while, just as everyone else's problems will also disappear in time.

> What is your favourite way of getting some perspective?
>
> What reminds you that this too shall pass?
>
> And how does that help?

Four very helpful words to deal with extreme pressure

One of my favourite mindset stories comes from the Australian 400m runner Cathy Freeman. At the Sydney Olympics Freeman was the only home athlete with the chance of winning a medal on the track. There was a lot of focus and pressure on her, to say the least.

To add to the pressure she was given the torch to light the Olympic flame at the opening ceremony and, as an indigenous Australian, she felt she was representing not only her country but her people too.

She reached the final of the 400 metres and, in her warm up, kept repeating what she later described as "four very simple words". They were "do what I know".

"Do what I know" is a great example of simple, really effective, helpful 'self-talk' (the conversations we have with ourselves in our own heads). It's short, memorable, easily repeatable and powerful because it means something to her. It means 'I know the training that I've done, I know what I'm capable of, and I just need to 'do what I know'.'

And she did what she knew.

And she won.

Self-talk can be really helpful, but sometimes we can find ourselves repeating the wrong messages to ourselves. It's easy to find ourselves focusing on what we should do, or what others think, or about how things could go wrong. If we don't take the time to focus on what we should be telling ourselves, we can slip into bad habits quite quickly.

What happens when you stop and listen to your self-talk?

Are you keeping it simple and reminding yourself of what is important?

Or are you channelling your inner critic (or someone else's criticism) and questioning yourself?

If it's the latter, what happens when you try telling yourself Cathy Freeman's "Do what I know" line?

How do you respond to something like that?

And what does that response tell you about what you need to focus on?

Make your self-talk believable to you

I once coached a chap, Simon, who was just at the end of his first year in an MD role. Things were going well. Supported by his HR manager he arranged to get some feedback from the staff on his first 12 months of leadership.

Overall the picture was positive and people believed he was doing a good job. One criticism however that came through, was that he wasn't seen as particularly caring towards people.

As we discussed his goal(s) for the coaching I asked him "which is it, to care more about people or to be seen to care more about people?"

With typical honesty he replied "either will do"!

When we discussed this further and begin to develop a plan he decided that to tell himself he was becoming more caring about people simply didn't feel true. Instead, what did feel true, was to say that he was becoming more interested in people. This recognition helped him to be more curious, to ask more questions, and to try and understand people better. The assumption was that this would help him to become more empathetic.

Self-talk is a term used to describe the conversations we have with ourselves in our own heads. Our internal dialogue. Much like a coach or manager's words need to be credible to be believable - to have any positive impact - our own words to ourselves need to be the same.

When they are positive, useful and believable, they can be extremely helpful.

If you've watched the TV series Ted Lasso, you'll know that Coach Ted tapes a very basic handwritten sign over the door in the changing room, saying simply; 'Believe.' At first the players laugh at it and find it hard to take it seriously. Over time, as they begin to understand what Ted offers and how that can help them, they take the sign more seriously and come to value it.

We've all heard mantras or self-talk phrases that others find helpful. It's unusual that someone else's will work for you without some rephrasing to make it resonate for you, unless you have a clear understanding of the meaning behind it. Sometimes taking someone else's suggestion as a foundation to build your own meaning on can make all the difference, just like it did for the new MD Jim worked with.

What do you find it helpful to tell yourself?

How do you make it believable?

Suspend your ego and focus on what you can do

A few years ago I took part in a single day coast to coast cycling event from Seascale on the west coast of Cumbria across the country to Whitby on the north sea (about 150 miles).

On a couple of longer training rides I came to clearly realise that, for me, the event was all about stamina and completion rather than times.

For as long as I can remember, whenever I've been cycling, if someone has overtaken me there has been an urge to chase them and try and keep up or catch up. But on the long training rides I realised this was a pretty stupid thing to do!

I reminded myself that the rider overtaking me could be younger, fitter (maybe they didn't have a full-time job and trained like a professional), maybe they were an ex professional, and maybe they were just fitter, stronger and quicker than me at that time.

But whatever the reason, I had to tell my ego and my mind to keep quiet and to just let them go.

Your ego can be a help or a hindrance.

For several years I lived near a train station that had a steep set of stairs to and from the platforms. They could get fairly crowded when a train let off passengers, and unless you were there first you would have a slow journey out of the station as the crowd exiting would naturally move fairly ponderously up the stairs. At rush hour this often resulted in a pile of people waiting at the train doors nearest the exit, and the first people off the train would often race up the stairs to avoid getting caught up and slowed down by those behind. It was an unofficial competition to get up these steps first and win the 'race off the train' and I was a keen participant, relishing the occasions when I 'won'.

After a few years living there, I had a number of concussions that finished my rugby career and could barely walk for six weeks – I was staggering around like I'd had far too many drinks. When I had to go into London for appointments, getting up those steps to exit the station became an endurance test rather than a race as I would have to use the handrail to pull myself up rather than rely on my legs to do the work. Instead of trying to get up the steps first, I was waiting until most people had left the platform so I could get to the top in my own time.

If I'd told myself a few months before that I wouldn't be able to be the first to get up those stairs, I might have been frustrated and disappointed. My ego and desire to compete and win would have been infuriated. Yet when it came to it, it didn't really matter whether I was first or last, because getting to the top was all that I needed to achieve.

How often does your ego kick in when it doesn't need to?

Does it really help you?

The risks of trying really hard to be perfect

Bob Rotella's fantastic book Golf Is Not A Game Of Perfect has an unusual title. And while it's about golf, the stories and points he makes can be applied to many other areas of life. I read it when I was working as a Sales Trainer and I reckoned I could substitute the word Sales for Golf and most of it would make complete sense.

In the book he talks about how professional golfers, who are so good, practice so hard, and are so consistent, might reasonably expect to hit a course record every time they play. After all it's a closed skill, the ball is not moving and they're not being tackled when they make their shots.

However the reality is that it is not that easy. It's a small ball, being hit a long way with a long lever and so the margins for error are big. That's why it's a tough game – ask any amateur who is both capable of hitting the ball really well with a superbly timed stroke and might still play a totally duff shot the next minute.

Rotella says in the book that for these reasons, for the golfer who wants to work towards their potential, "striving for perfection is essential but demanding perfection is deadly".

This is such a great line and so true. Working hard to do your best at something is often an excellent strategy if you want to get better at it and do well. But demanding higher standards of yourself than you're capable of – in effort, technique or consistency – is a recipe for disaster.

As a rugby player, I was determined to be the best player I could be, and would devour books and documentaries about rugby players and other sporting figures. Often these great athletes would talk about training when conditions were tough and pushing yourself to be better than your opposition, whether that be stealing a march on someone by training on Christmas Day because you were sure they wouldn't be, or by going out running in the snow because everyone else would be at home staying warm.

Because I'd absorbed these books as guidance to becoming the best player I could be, I would regularly annoy my family by going for a run or bike ride on Christmas day when they wanted to be opening presents. I'd surprise walkers in the local park as I'd be out running in the snow in shorts and a t-shirt because no-one else would be that foolhardy. Although in retrospect they may have been more shocked by the concept of someone running so slowly but taking it so seriously!

Did it make any difference, pushing myself to go to another level? Probably not, to be honest. What I didn't really understand or want to acknowledge was that I wasn't at a level of athleticism where those incremental efforts would make a tangible difference to my performance. However, what it did do was ensure I felt that I'd left nothing behind in my efforts to be the best I could be, and that was what mattered to me at the time.

When have you pushed yourself harder than you needed to in pursuit of perfection?

Did it help?

Or would you have been better to slow down a little and see the bigger picture?

Responding to pressure with helpful self-talk

Everyone can feel pressure and experiences their confidence going up and down.

In Steve Redgrave's autobiography A Golden Age he talks about his experience prior to rowing the final in his 5th Olympic Games. He was already a gold medal winning rower four times in each of the previous four Olympics.

He talks about a moment, two hours before his final race, where he was suddenly hit by self-doubt and found himself questioning what he was doing there. He said that at that moment, if a helicopter had flown in and had room to take one person away, he would have fought people for the spot.

As it was, there was no helicopter, and he gave himself a good talking to, reminding himself he chose to be there, why he was there, what he was doing and of all the preparation etc that he had done. He had the proverbial 'word with himself' and gave himself the proverbial 'slap round the face'.

But self-doubt, and variable confidence, are both very normal things, even for the elite. And when these creep or spring upon us there are helpful ways we can respond.

I've noticed that one of the ways I respond to severe pressure at work is to think about winning the National Lottery. I don't buy tickets often – except when the pressure feels impossible and the idea of winning the lottery offers me a tantalising glimpse of a quick escape from the challenges I'm facing. Naturally I haven't won(!) but I often wonder if the distraction and fantasy thinking that the ticket purchase offers are a way of feeling in control of a difficult situation that feels impossible to influence.

It's really fascinating to read about Steve Redgrave looking for that same quick escape - albeit via helicopter – when faced with pressure, despite having faced similar pressures for his whole sporting career. Talking himself out of his self-doubt and reminding himself of all the reasons he was good enough was enough to put him back in control.

How do you respond to feeling that you're not in control in challenging or high-pressured situations?

Do you fantasise about a way to escape – whether being whisked away in a helicopter or winning the lottery?

What helps you feel in control and confident again?

Be careful that a negative future you see for yourself doesn't cloud your judgement

I was once working with someone, as part of a team, who was offered and decided to take, a bigger role which included regular international travel. It was likely to mean one long haul flight per month and quite a bit of time away from home, away from family.

When the person and I discussed the new role, they painted a picture of a job that they would probably do for a couple of years, that would be great for their CV, great for their experience, but which they probably wouldn't do for any longer than two years because they would be knackered. And they envisioned hotel life would not be great for their waistline.

I had a different perspective, and the difference was fascinating, so we went on to discuss it. The person was slightly overweight and not as fit and healthy as they would like to be. So we talked about a vision where at the end of two years they got all the positives of taking the role and were also fitter and healthier. We talked about the opportunity to make that happen and how they would do it, including things like hotel gyms, walking, and how they could make helpful food choices.

In reality it was simple stuff, based on recognising an unhelpful vision of the future, replacing it with something much closer to ideal – ideal but still possible - and putting in place a simple plan.

It can be hard to change our habits; once we have a routine, we tend to stick to it and make plans around it. Whether they're good habits is an interesting question!

Tim Harford's book Messy is a fascinating read about how to be creative. One of the points he makes is that disruption can drive change in our habits, and he uses the example of a Tube strike. In 2012 there was a 48 hour tube strike, and the journeys that commuters took before and after the strike were compared using Oyster card data. Tens of thousands of commuters permanently changed their route after the strike – but the new travel methods and routes they were using had been available before the strike, they had just never considered changing their routine. Being forced to try something new had uncovered unexpected benefits.

Just like Jim's colleague, how often do you use a change to review your habits and routines?

Does changing your routine become easier if you're already making a change in your life? What helps you adapt to making a change?

You don't need to be ready until you need to be ready

One of my children played a good level of schoolboy rugby. He was in an excellent year group which really helped. He went on play a first full season of adult rugby as an 18-year-old. He liked much about the game – the team work, the team spirit and the fitness - but he wasn't the sort who got out of bed on matchday fired up and ready to go.

Often as we got in the car to drive to the club he might say "I don't feel up for it today". I would reply that he didn't need to feel up for it at that moment in time but when the whistle went for the start of the game. And that's what the warm up was for.

We would repeat that conversation on many Saturdays until it almost didn't need saying. At least not in full.

When you're thinking ahead to something, maybe nervous, maybe worried, remember you don't need to feel ready until you need to be ready. And you can use the time between whenever now is and the event itself to get as ready as you can. (And at that point do your best with whatever you have).

You don't need to be 'up for it' all the time. For many of us that would be exhausting.

Not long before my rugby career was ended by too many concussions, I remember questioning whether I was properly mentally prepared for a game because I wasn't nervous. I had always felt that an element of nerves before a match showed I was taking the unknown seriously, and that I could use the pressure I felt to fuel my performance – the nerves would get me up for it and I would be ready to play.

Not feeling nervous made me question whether I would be able to perform at my best when the match started. In fact, not feeling nervous probably made me more worried than when I had felt a little on edge before the game!

> How do nerves help you? Do they make you feel as if you won't be able to perform, or do you feel they'll help you be your best?
>
> How do you manage your worries ahead of something big happening?

Understanding and avoiding thinking errors and thinking loops

My friend Lou Macari (the Lou Macari, not his cousin the famous ex-footballer) introduced me to Thinking Errors. These are unhelpful patterns of thinking that people sometimes do (and are common enough to be given names) like catastrophisation, mis-labelling or all-or-nothing thinking. They were introduced to me as Thinking Errors though I've since heard them called other things including, more correctly, cognitive distortions.

On the list Lou showed me there were seven or eight of them with an instruction to:
- See if you recognise any of them as ones that you do
- Test the evidence for your thinking – is there good reason to be thinking this way or are you making a 'thinking error'
- Work to replace unfounded or unhelpful thoughts with more realistic or helpful ones

I'd add one of my own to the original list, which is thinking loops – getting stuck in patterns of thinking that go round and round unhelpfully without going anywhere productive.

As an example, one of my children had a friend in primary school whose Mum, a single parent, was dying of cancer. It was a pretty tragic situation and for a while there was no obvious place where the child would live and who would look after him. Our home was one of the possible options, along with a couple of other families who would have looked after him if it came to it. In the end he went to live with cousins.

But for a long time, when it wasn't obvious what would happen, my thinking about what might happen kept coming back to "if only his Mum didn't have cancer". This was such an unhelpful place to get to – because she did have cancer! And it looked highly unlikely that she was going to get better.

Eventually I recognised the thinking loop and got better at heading it off, by asking myself a more useful question like "what can we do?" or reassuring myself that there were enough good people involved that there would be a solution somehow. In the end a relative of the child took him in.

Watch out for thinking errors and thinking loops!

Recently I had to give a big presentation at work to some very important people. I hadn't had much experience of working with those people but I knew they could be very critical and demanded a lot from anyone who worked with them. I was incredibly nervous because I wanted to make a good impression and was really concerned that my job would be at risk if I didn't do well.

I mentioned this to a colleague in passing, and they challenged me, asking me what was the worst that could happen, especially given that my boss wouldn't just let someone else say I should be out of a job without challenging it!

They were right, of course, but even though I knew that it was unlikely to actually be the outcome in the event that the presentation didn't go well, I was still really worried about it. I was totally stuck in the thinking loop and focusing on my perception of the audience rather than the quality and value of my work.

Of course, when it came to it, it all seemed to go smoothly. All of that worrying had probably helped me do a good job, but wasn't really necessary.

How do you recognise when you are in a thinking error or loop?

What helps you understand what is happening and how do you find a route out of the pattern?

Thinking that you are something increases the chances that you will be!

Many years ago I worked on a training team with a lovely guy called Steve Williams. He once went on a week-long creative thinking course. (He or our boss must have either thought his creative thinking really needed to improve or we had a lot of unallocated budget to send people on a week-long course! I'm not sure week-long residential courses for creative thinking still exist).

When Steve got back to the office I asked him what he had learnt. He replied "if you think you're creative you will be". I think I was both surprised and dissatisfied with his answer, so I asked him what he meant. "For example," he said, "if I'm going to a do a brainstorm, now I'll say to myself "I'm going to come up with more ideas than anyone else – no matter about their quality – and keep going longer than anyone else"".

As it happens, I didn't consider myself creative back then, so I gave his tips a go and they_worked for me.

I guess it depends on your definition of creative. I rarely come up with original ideas, but I'm good at remembering things, so when someone asks me for creative ideas, or other ways of doing things, I can sometimes come up with things they've never thought of.

Creative?

Back when I was on a cohort of 'performance champions' working with Jim, I was experiencing some difficult moments in my personal life. Friends from the cohort were incredibly supportive, and I asked one how he was always so positive. He told me to "fake it until you believe it." I gave it a go, and it seemed to work, so I tried to keep it up.

One morning a few months later I was walking into the office and bumped into him outside. I gave him a cheery "Good morning!" and a huge grin, and he commented on how happy I seemed. I told him that I wasn't feeling that great at all before saying good morning, but that "fake it until you believe it" really did work!

> Have you ever tried to believe you are positive, or happy, or creative?
>
> What happened?

Ideas for idea generation

For a few years I belonged to a group called the Sales Training Association who would have quarterly meetings that I would sometimes attend, depending on the agenda. It wasn't a big group with something around 15 to 20 people at each gathering.

One session was about problem solving. We were split into four groups of about five people. One person in each group was asked to share with the group a problem that they were working on and wanted to solve.

We then moved in our groups around four different stations for five minutes at a time. One station was a classic brainstorm task to come up with ideas. In another we had to use analogies and metaphors ("it sounds a bit like…" or "your problem reminds me of…") to see what solutions they conjured up. Another station involved looking at the problem using a different perspective and famous people (what would Donald Trump do? Or Madonna? Or Harry Potter? And the other station, my favourite (though I thought they were all good), involved putting on a hat and playing instruments together – maracas, toy trumpet etc) with a very deliberate aim to forget the problem for a few minutes and then, at the end, asking for ideas. Random, but it worked!

I've tried all these methods since and I think they all have a place.

Alternatively, as recently discovered, if you are looking for ways to come up with ideas, ask Chat GPT.

One of my favourite pieces of advice for anyone experiencing negative self-talk is to imagine that someone you really dislike (and would never listen to in a million years) is telling you those things.

For example, if you find your inner narrative telling you that you're lazy because you slept late at the weekend when you could have been doing chores, would you pay any attention to those words if they came from e.g. Donald Trump, or Uncle Scar from the Lion King?
If you wouldn't put up with that awful person telling you those things, why listen to them at all?

What happens when you take different perspectives and try out new approaches on a problem?

What works best for you?

Having a can do attitude can create opportunities

What is scary or foolish for one person is an opportunity for another.

I was once working as part of a Sales Training team when into our office walked a lady, Sue,_who had moved from sales, into sales training, and back to sales again. Also in the room was a colleague, Gary – Scottish, and a keen golfer.

Sue was exuberant, outgoing and energetic and she started telling us about a customer team meeting she had recently been presenting at down in the south east of England. It had been a group that she had been trying to get to see for a while and so at the end she was delighted when they asked her back.

As she was leaving them one of the team explained that they usually followed their monthly team meetings with a round of golf, and asked her if she played and if she would like to join them next time. "I'd love to", Sue had replied.

Gary and I looked at each other, horrified and intrigued in equal measure. "And do you? Play?" he asked, slightly nervously. "No," said Sue, her head slightly reversing off her shoulders (in the words of Bill Bryson), "but how hard can it be?"

Gary and I looked at each other, again, and he spoke first. We both had images of her hacking her way around a tough 18-hole course, taking divots out of the greens, holding up other players and risking making a fool of herself.

"Well, you'll have to tell them" he said, "that you can't play". I had similar thoughts, but, because it was Sue, and not wanting to dampen her enthusiasm, I simply offered to practice with her, on the local pay-as-you-play par 3 course.

I did practice with her and, as a hockey player, she already had a good swing and an eye for the ball. In the end she did play with her customer a few months later and though she wasn't brilliant by then she was totally fine.

To me the story epitomises the proverbial "can do" attitude. It also prompted me (through a roundabout route) to buy The Inner Game of Golf – which I gave to Sue - and Bob Rotella's Golf Is Not A Game Of Perfect which I read (and which, as the first book I'd ever read by a sports psychologist, was life changing).

A few years later Sue had a change of job role and moved to Bermuda. Not long after arriving she was walking around a marina and got chatting to a skipper who was looking for a third crew member to sail his yacht back to the UK. Sue volunteered and helped crew the boat home, despite no sailing experience. "How hard can it be?" I imagine she was thinking.

I often feel quite lucky that I happened to go to an all-girls high school. It meant that I never experienced anyone telling me that I couldn't do something because I was a girl.

At the same time I was a member of my local air cadets squadron – which was very small – which gave me amazing opportunities, particularly to try rifle shooting and flying. No-one ever told me that I couldn't do something because I was a girl, even if I was the only girl there at times.

Many years later, I'd regularly head off on my own for holidays, especially to the USA where I could combine photography trips to a National Park with some time visiting family on the East Coast. I remember being at a big family dinner with them at the end of one trip, and someone admiring my bravery in hiring a car and exploring a National Park alone.

I was surprised, as it didn't seem brave or even a big thing to me – in fact, there didn't seem to be any reason why I shouldn't do it.

> What have you done because there didn't seem to be any reason why you shouldn't do it?
>
> What happens when you dive into something because you think you will be able to do it, or learn to do it, like Sue?

Gary Player and his favourite greens – loving wherever you are

A story I've heard a couple of times, in different formats, is about responses to conditions.

The first time I heard it was in Bob Rotella's Golf Is Not A Game Of Perfect – a book mentioned earlier. He tells of the young South African golfer Gary Player starting to make his way on the American professional golf circuit in the 1950s and room sharing with a young Davis Love Jr.

The two youngsters play on a course down in the deep South in the States where the greenkeeper has left the Bermuda grass very long so the greens are really slow to putt on, like putting on a shag pile carpet. Davis Love struggled but after each of the four rounds Player talked about how much he loved the slow, Bermuda grass greens.

A couple of weeks later the pair played in the north of the country where the course_superintendent had the bent grass cut so short it was like putting on linoleum. Once again Player raved, this time about how much he loves the super-fast greens.

Love couldn't stand the contradiction, so turned to Player and said "which is it Gary? Do you love slow Bermuda greens or fast, bent greens?"

"You just have to love whichever greens you're playing on," Player replied. So true.

When I was younger, I never wanted to work in London. It was too big, too noisy, too built up and grey. I wanted to spend my time in the countryside. Ironic then, that I've lived in and on the outskirts of London since finishing my undergraduate degree, studied for two masters degrees in the city, and commuted into the centre for several jobs. I've also commuted by car for a number of years to a job further out of the city, and I've worked from home.

Being one of the older siblings in my family, I've often talked to my younger brother and sister about job opportunities and applications. At times they've insisted that they wouldn't want to work in London, or commute more than 15 minutes by car, or on a train. And I've always told them that it's not as bad as they think it will be; that however you end up getting to work, you find a way to make it pleasant, and you'll come to value how you spend that time.

When I was small and visiting my grandparents, my Grandpa would spend half an hour every morning – often with his breakfast on a tray – sitting looking out of the lounge window in silence. Us kids were absolutely not to go near him or disturb his peace and quiet. He had learned to love the quiet thoughtful moments of his commute so much that he found a way to replicate that time after he had retired.

How do you find a way to love the conditions you're in?

What helps you make the adjustment, and how do you hold onto what you gain as you adapt?

Looking after your own thinking

An Ironman Triathlon is a big undertaking. A few years ago I knew a group of about a dozen local runners, swimmers, cyclists who had entered their first Ironman – in Sherborne, Dorset (including Sandra, Garry, Selina, Jo, Mark, Alan, Richard...).

I became really interested in what they were taking on and asked how much training they were doing? "Lots" they said. I then asked how much mental prep they were doing? And I got blank looks.

So we all got together for four sessions of "mental prep". Most of it was basic planning – how do I want to feel mentally on the start line? What's my mental response when someone swims over me or I get a puncture? What are my gold, silver and bronze goals?

They liked the idea that of all the thousands of starters on the day they could be better mentally prepared than anyone else.

I asked in session 1 how much time they were spending mentally preparing and they said: "not a lot". At that point, one of them, Alan – the only one who'd completed an ironman before – said "that's not true! I bet you're thinking about it all the time!"

Which was pretty accurate.

Only their thinking wasn't always conscious and it wasn't always helpful. This was something we were quite quickly able to make progress with. Replacing unhelpful thoughts with more helpful ones and choosing helpful responses to predictable possible scenarios.

I was once chatting to a colleague who had a family member stuck in a hotel abroad with a hurricane bearing down on them. The colleague's sibling was very frightened, and they explained that as they were unable to do anything that would help get the sibling out of the situation, they had discussed how the sibling might feel when the hurricane hit.

Trying to get them to visualise what the situation would look like, sound and feel like, and how they might deal with the noises and fear was the most practical way to help in that situation.
It helped the sibling to panic less and made the experience a bit less stressful by focusing their thoughts on what the experience would actually be like, rather than just their fear.

When have you used visualisation or tried to find helpful thoughts to navigate a new or challenging situation?

How was it helpful?

---

11 SUPPORT

"None of us are as smart as all of us" (or "everybody is cleverer than anybody")

TALLEYRAND

Support can be, at the right time, of immense value. If you are interested in performing at your best then valuing and using the support available to you will be crucial – whether you are going well or at times when you are struggling.

If anything it's a trait of young males to feel they don't need support. Older males have learnt that this is not true! Just a few stories here to illustrate this.

Having the support of others to help you stay in control

Many years ago I worked with an enthusiastic, friendly young chap who, having started in a sales support job, landed a role as a sales consultant, visiting customers and loving his work. He had done really well to progress quickly, at a young age, to the job he was in.

Then one day, out of the blue for him, the rug got pulled from under his feet. Returning from a holiday with his girlfriend he got a message to report on Monday morning to a local hotel. There in the foyer he met his manager, the regional manager and someone from HR. As they went up in the lift to a meeting room on an upper floor he turned to his manager and said "This isn't a normal monthly 1-1 is it?". His role, along with many others, was redundant.

This was tough for him. Unlike some of his peers in the salesforce - some older, some more experienced, some better networked in the business - he had not seen it coming at all.

Over the following weeks many people supported him mentally, emotionally and practically. One colleague, Barry, and I, were particularly directive with him, between us checking in most days, telling him to stay active, to get up, shave, dress, go out, call recruitment agents, go for a walk, visit a museum, keep in touch.

Eventually of course he got another job but it was a tough time when he wasn't necessarily equipped to cope on his own. As often we're not.

Everyone needs support and to feel sufficiently autonomous.

When I was younger, I decided that when I wrote a book I would list the names of everyone who had helped and supported me at any point, to show my gratitude. As I've got older, I've realised that the list of names would be a book in itself.

Isn't that wonderful, to have encountered so many amazing people who would give me their time, advice, support, or lend a friendly ear? It says something remarkable about our fellow humans, that despite what the news or social media would have you believe, that people really do care about those around them, and will do anything to make life easier for someone they know.

And in that way, as much as it would be nice to write a book just listing all of those names (maybe I should become an artist and call it art instead), I've realised that the best way to show my gratitude is to pay that support and kindness forward into the world.

Who would you thank for supporting you when you needed a hand?

And who has been grateful to you for your kindness in helping them?

The value of support through difficulty

When I was in my late 40s I got divorced. It was unplanned, unpleasant and a time of great discomfort. It was complicated, emotional and there were many points when I, along with others, felt out of control of what was happening.

Whilst I wouldn't want to go through it again - not least because of the pain it caused for others - I look at it as a life experience that I've had. Even when going through it - unclear what was going to happen next, trying to put myself in others' shoes, trying to think about my children and lessening the impact on them - I found myself occasionally able to step back from the drama and, briefly, see it objectively. This enabled me during those moments to try not be a victim or a persecutor but an observer.

I think two things enabled me to do this. One was a personality that allows a level of detachment and some emotional control, but the other, far bigger factor, was the support I had from two people. One a work colleague and one an old friend. Both listened and were non-judgmental. Both cared about me and others involved. One in particular occasionally told me things straight that I needed to hear. The other in particular helped me gain perspective by playing back what he was hearing, often by comparing to something else like a film or other storyline.

Their support was invaluable in not only working through all the aspects of divorce but also helping me to keep going with work and life during that period. I'm glad that they were there and that I was able to benefit from their wisdom and advice.

I'm lucky enough not to have experienced the pain of a divorce, as Jim has. Of course, everyone has challenging, uncomfortable and emotionally turbulent periods in their life and feeling supported is such a vital component in both getting through the situation and being able to process it in a healthy way.

I stopped playing rugby in 2011 after a series of concussions that left me unable to walk very well for several weeks. I managed to recover from the initial injuries and returned to work, but found my health and cognitive abilities deteriorated significantly in the following months. After a lot of medical appointments and tests, the following summer I received a letter saying my lumbar puncture results warranted an appointment with the consultant neurologist whilst simultaneously saying I was discharged from his clinic! When I saw the neurologist to discuss the results he was clearly not interested in my case, told me I was lucky not to have a terminal illness and to go and live my life as there was nothing wrong with me. It was a particularly soul-destroying moment because his professional opinion meant no-one believed me when I said something was wrong.

Eventually I got a second opinion, received treatment for serious vitamin deficiencies and recovered well enough to gradually resume my life and return to exercise.

After such an awful experience, finding that I had developed a new and unexplored chronic illness ten years later turned out to be an amazing contrast. The doctors believed me, listened to my symptoms and tried to help. They never dismissed me or tried to get rid of me. I was also connected to a huge community of fellow sufferers going through similar experiences as me. It meant I never felt alone as I always had someone to talk to about what I was going through, and I could listen to others and sympathise with anyone who felt unheard. My past experiences helped me to advocate for the patient community, and I knew that if I ever needed help, others would help advocate for me.

Feeling supported meant I was able to keep going with life as best I could, even with the new limitations on my life.

> When have you felt heard and supported through a
> challenging time?
>
> What helped you feel connected to others?
>
> What made the biggest difference to you?

The value in hearing it straight from a friend

One time I was pretty unhappy with some aspects of my employer and I decided to look around. I applied for a training job with a national charity and got a first interview. The salary was just over half what I was currently on and this came up in the first interview.

My partner was supportive but I could tell she had reservations. The same too with my financial adviser friend. I mentioned it to one or two other trusted people because it felt like a big decision. Then I had a text message from another friend which said "Don't do it. It's not nice to feel poor."

I was surprised by the directness from this particular friend but I found it really helpful. It kind of shocked me into a new perspective and at that point I pretty much decided to withdraw from the selection process.

A few hours later I had a second message from the same friend which said "Sorry about that. I was at the gate about to board a plane so I didn't have time to write a longer message. It feels like a good opportunity but it's too soon. I think you should wait."

I contacted the charity and withdrew my application, with my apologies – and to the relief of my financial adviser friend and most of all my partner.

I know I learnt how useful it had been to get some honest, timely, direct and succinct advice from a trusted friend.

I once applied for a graduate job with a very high-profile top-notch advertising agency that would have involved doing some work on their intranet. The first few months of the role would have entailed tidying up existing files and content, before starting the interesting element of the work. I went along for an interview and had a great chat with the potential line manager and came away feeling hopeful.

I heard back pretty quickly, with the feedback from the recruiting manager being surprisingly direct; he felt I would be bored in the role, especially in the first few months, and thought it unfair to take me on for it. He added that he was going to revise the job specification as the interview had shown him that he needed to think more about what was needed for the organisation.

A different source of direct and timely advice, but still ultimately useful, and also correct – I would have been bored very quickly!

> When have you been given direct but invaluable advice, and how did it help you?
>
> Have you ever been so direct with someone else?

12 TEAMS

"If you want to build a ship, don't drum up people to collect wood and don't assign them tasks and work, but rather teach them to long for the endless immensity of the sea."

ANTOINE DE SAINT-EXUPÉRY

"The strength of the wolf is in the pack and the strength of the pack is in the wolf."

KIPLING

"If you want to go fast, go alone; if you want to go far, go together."

AFRICAN PROVERB

"If everyone is moving forward together, then success takes care of itself."

HENRY FORD

It seems clear to me that many organisations appear to focus on, value, develop and reward individuals more than they do teams. This has never made sense to me.

Given the number of teams I have been in and coached it surprises me that there are not more stories in this section. But everyone I have told a story about elsewhere was part of a team! And great teams are, ultimately, made of great individuals.

A team needs to be united and aligned

To perform anywhere near its best a team needs to be aligned - in a direction or towards a goal.

I was once working with a team where one of the members, a lady, with some bravery and at slight risk to herself said "I don't feel like we're united. I don't think we're all united on this team:. To which one of her male colleagues responded "no, I think we are".

The conversation started to move on before I interjected to say that we couldn't let that exchange pass without understanding it and resolving it. My instinct was that the male colleague was not very understanding, and didn't care too much if the lady didn't feel united. He did and that was of greater concern to him!

Aligning together, and being united, is at the essence of being a team.

I was once leading a team that I felt was pretty united, and that we all understood the needs of the team and how things worked most effectively. I was very surprised one day when a team member asked for something that I felt was very obviously not going to work for the team, and that I wouldn't be able to give them. They were not happy with the situation and took it very personally, despite my best efforts to explain why it wouldn't work and attempting to find a solution that met them halfway.

It can be easy to forget that not everyone on the team has the same experiences or perspective as you do. It isn't always easy to 'stop the boat' and truly find out what is working well and correcting course on the areas that aren't in alignment. But it is definitely worth it.

> When have you been surprised by a lack of alignment in the team?
>
> What helped you understand the problem and find ways to fix it?

Team purpose needs to be clear, shared, meaningful and memorable

Clearly, knowing the purpose of the team that you are part of, can really make a difference to your motivation and your work.

I worked with a team in an insurance company. They were a team of specialists who would get work referred to them by other frontline, customer facing teams. Shortly after I started working with them another team doing the same work merged with them to make a larger team of about 15 or 16 people.

I asked them how confident they were, on a scale of 1 to 10, that if they each wrote down the purpose of the team they would all write down the same thing? I've asked this question of dozens and dozens of teams and, unless the team happened to have very recently discussed it, the typical response is laughter and shaking of heads and disagreement. This team was typical but, as a team of largely introverts, there was minimal laughter or expression!

So I asked them to each write down the purpose of the team and, actually, they were remarkably similar. They all wrote something broadly along the lines of "to efficiently deal_with specialist technical queries". Strictly speaking this was a pretty accurate and true description of what they did. But the reason for asking the team purpose question was to improve motivation. So I asked them what would give them pride and satisfaction in their work? What purpose, if they looked back, would make them think "I was part of the team that did, or achieved, that"?

After some discussion, that only lasted about 20 minutes, they came up with a purpose that was three words, rather than a sentence. They decided that their purpose was to "Perform, Educate and Inspire". By this they meant:

- Perform: do our jobs well, to the best of our abilities, as a team and meet our targets
- Educate: train others how to deal with some of the more specialist queries that currently get passed to us
- Inspire: show others, or allow them to see, the things we are doing as a team to improve - and how - so that they might want to do some of the same

This made a huge difference to the team, and they went from strength to strength. Individuals learned and the team learned together. They had decided themselves to do what they wanted to do and it was exactly what the more senior leaders in the business would have wanted them to do if they had been telling them. It was win, win, win for everyone concerned.

I've often worked in organisations that have defined values, or principles, or mission statements, for their staff body. I've always assumed that if, like the team Jim mentions, you were part of the group that defines the values or principles, that they will have great meaning for you and help you feel part of the wider team and staff community. I've also felt that if you aren't part of the group creating these statements – whether you weren't included or joined after they were set – that the words won't hold much meaning for you.

This is often compounded by appraisal forms requiring staff to self-assess how well they meet the organisational values. If you don't feel connected to those words, every self-assessment is a little alienating and a reminder that they don't mean as much to you as to others.

How do you solve this problem organisationally? Do you regularly re-evaluate your values and principles with new working groups? Do you raise team purpose above organisational values and ensure teams regularly do as Jim's client team did, and set and review their team purpose to allow everyone to feel a valued part of their own team, and therefore playing their part in the wider organisation? Or do you ask your original participants to act as evangelists and work with the wider staff group and new starters to help them feel connected to the values, principles and purpose of the organisation?

What has worked for you in teams you've been part of?

What helped you all feel part of the team, moving in the same direction?

The newish team without a clear purpose

There are many teams in organisations who aren't really, collectively clear on why they exist.

Newly formed teams are an exception, but even then it might be that the bosses who created the team are clearer, or have a different understanding, than the team members themselves.

I once worked with a team in a global insurance business. They had a few full-time team members, including the team leader, but the rest were based around the world reporting via their geographic region. It was a big team of about 20-25 people so when we all met in the UK I asked them why they existed and there was far from complete clarity.

After a short discussion of about 30 minutes, and input from everyone, they recognised that collaboration was so important to the success of the team that they included it in why they existed, not just how they needed to operate.

And they recognised that they could easily get distracted by or tempted to prioritise things in their local area. So they decided that the reason they existed was "to relentlessly collaborate to underwrite bigger risks". They were happy. But after a break we came back into the room and they acknowledged that they were doing this to steal a march on other businesses, so they added at the end "to beat the competition". Now they were really happy.

"to relentlessly collaborate to underwrite bigger risks, to beat the competition". They had nailed it and it made a big difference to them.

Ben Hunt-Davies and Hilary Beveridge give another superb example of a clear team mission in Will It Make The Boat Go Faster.

And personally, I don't get too hung up on whether we're talking team mission, purpose, team goal or why the team exists. For practical purposes they can feel so much the same, so long as there's a simple, clear, memorable answer. Rather than spending time discussing the definition or semantics, you're better off just answering the question.

I mentioned earlier that I started playing rugby by joining a new/re-forming team in a small town in New Zealand. The local league included well-established teams with experienced international players, and so we had a clear mission for the season: beat the one team in the league who were worse than us. No other game mattered, so we had plenty of freedom to make mistakes and learn from them in order to put in the right performance in the two games we could win.

Having a clear purpose or raison d'etre is very liberating and allows everyone to pull together. I've been in teams where either the mission wasn't clear, or perhaps it felt like some work was pulling in a different direction (for good reason). Not being clear that the part you play adds value, or having to push to have that confirmed by your leaders, is pretty dispiriting. You end up focusing on proving you belong or that you add value, rather than doing what you're there to do.

What teams have you been part of that made you feel confused about why you were there, or how to prove your value?

What was the difference between working in those situations, and working in a situation where you knew what you had to do and why?

How inclusivity is such a strong and important factor in teams

Competition within a team and team work can be highly compatible. As part of a dissertation I once studied the motives of under 11 youth football coaches and the motivational climate they create.

One manager in particular puzzled me but was the source of the richest learning. Using a questionnaire we established his competitiveness. At a 6-a-side tournament, over several games, he would pick his best team every time, even if it meant two squad players hardly got any time on the pitch.

But the questionnaires that the boys completed indicated that they all felt a strong part of the team.

The manager's values around inclusivity and everyone playing a part meant that he was able to instil a feeling that everyone was part of the team, and everyone had a part to play, even if they rarely played!

In certain circumstances being left out and feeling left out are different things.

At the moment, I'm working from home and not travelling into the office. My organisation is quite good at holding meetings online, so I don't really miss out on big things. However, occasionally things are set up as in-person only and I have to miss out.

The difference in how I feel about them is absolutely determined by the approach of the organiser. If they announce it is in person only, and don't acknowledge that not everyone will be able to go, it can feel quite isolating and exclusionist. If the announcement includes acknowledging that some people won't be able to attend and they can either get involved in a different way, or there is an invitation to discuss options for involvement with the organiser, then it feels very inclusive – even if I end up missing out.

How have you helped everyone in your teams feel included?

How have you approached situations where some people might miss out on an opportunity or an event? What made the difference?

Don't look to be perfect from day 1 in a new team

I like Chris Hadfield's story in his book "An Astronaut's Guide To Life On Earth".

As an astronaut, twice at the International Space Station, including one serving as commander, he knows a thing or two about teams and new team members joining teams.

In the book he says "in any new situation you will almost certainly be viewed in one of three ways. As a minus one: actively harmful, someone who creates problems. Or as a zero: your impact is neutral and doesn't tip the balance one way or other. Or you'll be seen as a plus one: someone who actively adds value. Everyone wants to be a plus one, of course. But proclaiming your plus one-ness at the outset almost guarantees you'll be perceived as a minus one, regardless of the skills you bring to the table or how you actually perform. This might seem self-evident, but it can't be, because so many people do it.

When you have some skills but don't fully understand your environment, there is no way you can be a plus one. At best you can be a zero. But a zero isn't a bad thing to be. You're competent enough not to create problems or make more work for everyone else. And you have to be competent, and prove to others that you are, before you can be extraordinary. There are no shortcuts, unfortunately."

So despite the enthusiasm, the ambition and the desire to contribute of the new person, setting out, to start with, to be a zero, might just be the best way to go.

I once started a new job where I was lucky enough to have a few days of handover with my predecessor, who had been in the role for several years. I watched her deal with all sorts of issues with complete ease, seeing that she knew the team and the work inside out. I then met up with my new boss, and tried to find a way to explain that although I wasn't familiar with those things yet, that I knew given time I would have the depth of knowledge and experience to be able to work in that calm, controlled manner too.

Like Jim's story, I knew I wasn't a plus one yet. But I also knew that I could become the plus one by watching, learning, and experiencing the challenges of the role and getting to know the team around me. I like to think that I did get there!

How have you managed to convey your enthusiasm to become a plus one without trying to present yourself as the finished article when joining a team?

If you had a new teammate or colleague, what would be the best thing they could say or do in order for you to see them as adding value – or working towards doing so?

Competitive collaboration – competing at being the best and the best at collaborating

Sales folk can be competitive. There is something about the rewards, and the ability to keep going, that marks them out as different. I have always enjoyed working with them because by and large their desire to get results means they are prepared to work at getting better. Hence, providing you are credible as a trainer/coach, and have something to offer, they are proactive at listening and putting things into practice.

I once worked with four regional teams who were nicely competitive with one another. Each trying to out produce the other and be top of the table.

After some work with each team, where each team decided their own team purpose, one team decided that they not only wanted to be the leading team but they wanted to be the best at collaborating with the other teams. Rarely(?), for a sales team, they could see the bigger picture, and that if all four teams were doing well it would be good for everyone.

Their philosophy was "we will share all our best ideas with you, and support you, but we will still beat you"!

I have come across competitive collaboration in other spheres too. The one I remember best is the British hurdler and world record holder, Colin Jackson, training with his number one rival, Canadian Mark McCoy. Their thinking was that they would push each other and both go faster as a result.

Competitive collaboration can be a highly effective applied concept.

I've worked in situations where people have got very 'territorial' over what they believe their role is, and if anyone else started an initiative or conversation that they felt they should have been leading, they complained. It made for a pretty awkward atmosphere, especially when teams weren't aware of that person's work or expertise.

As a team of one in my current specialism, I've tried to take the opposite approach. If I hear of someone doing something that might be within my remit, I try to encourage them and support it where I can, but I don't get upset. Firstly, I don't have the capacity to do everything, so if someone else is doing a great job I don't want to get in their way! And secondly, I might learn something from them by watching and supporting them. They can often be helping me achieve my objectives without even realising it!

When have you used collaboration and the efforts of other teams to your advantage?

How has that changed your perspective on success?

Abilene – talking about the unspoken that has not been talked about

You might have heard of Abilene – either because it's a place in Texas or because of the Abilene paradox which takes its name from the town.

The paradox is one you can look up, but to summarise, it's about a group of people agreeing to go somewhere that none of them want to go to. It's different to group think, which, according to Wikipedia, "occurs within a group of people in which the desire for harmony or conformity in the group results in an irrational or dysfunctional decision-making outcome... or the desire for cohesiveness may produce a tendency among its members to agree at all costs. This causes the group to minimize conflict and reach a consensus decision without critical evaluation."

I first came across the Abilene paradox when working as a business consultant alongside a respected and knowledgeable colleague, Lou Macari.

We were consulting with a business which had four shareholders. Two were the more experienced, driving decision making business owners and two were more of the engine room types but, from memory, the latter two were the two Directors. There was a reason, that I can't clearly remember, that meant the former two could not be Directors of the business for regulatory reasons.

But what I do remember is the skill and intuition of my colleague in diagnosing a problem. He kind of sensed it or sniffed it out. After our first meeting with them as a group he said that as part of our process of understanding their business he would like us to interview them separately.

It turned out, as he suspected, that the four of them had very different visions, aspirations and intentions for the business.

He made a plan to share our findings and recommendations back with them, the first part of which was to tell and explain the Abilene paradox. With that skilful positioning he was able to expose the gaps – or chasms – between their thinking and perspectives. It was a highly charged and emotional part of a tricky meeting. One of the four had to get up and leave the room because of what he had heard, for the first time, explaining later that stepping outside to gain some sort of composure was his only way of coping and not flying off into an angry rage.

Abilene is all about the management of agreement, rather than the management of disagreement, and its use as a story, to effect painful but necessary change, was great learning for me.

I once had a very awkward conversation with someone who worked for me.

They had excellent specialist expertise in an area which interested them and had worked hard to carve out a niche for themselves in putting that expertise into practice for the benefit of the wider organisation. At the time we had the conversation, they were keen to do more of this kind of work because they enjoyed it and felt it offered clear value.

Rather clumsily, I pointed out that whilst it was their main interest and area of expertise, the organisation was going through a number of changes which meant that the specialist element of their contribution was not valued and didn't command much engagement, despite the value it added. In addition, this specialist work was only a part of their role and the other parts were mission-critical for our team, so going forward they should focus less on the specialist area. I knew this would be disappointing for them, although at the time I didn't clearly envision the end result; they found a new role a couple of months later.

I wish I had had the skill of Jim and his colleague in using something like the Abilene paradox to explain that there was no point in me saying something I thought my colleague would like to hear if it wasn't true to the team and organisation's needs. Although what I said was correct in principle, communicating it more effectively could have softened the blow and enabled more of a conversation about short-term and longer-term organisational needs.

Have you ever had others struggle to be clear in their communication about the end-goal to you? Conversely, have they been abrupt and clear but not communicated well about the situation?

What has worked best for you, and how could you use a story like the Abilene paradox to help you communicate better in future?

---

13 ROLES IN TEAMS

Great things in business are never done by one person. They're done by a team of people."

STEVE JOBS

Having clarity on your role – what it is and what it isn't – and the roles of those around you, is pretty essential for teams that want to perform at their best. But so often this clarity, and in particular the shared clarity, is missing.

In teams the two most important factors seem to me to be 1. Purpose – direction, uniting, alignment and 2. Roles – clarity, flexibility, delivery.

Is it a personality clash or just a misunderstanding – through lack of clarity

I once coached a team where there was, what was described to me, a problem between two team members. It seemed like they didn't get on and there wasn't a great deal of professional respect.

One of them was quieter, serious, organised, introverted and not that expressive – except that his frustration was visible.

The other was talkative, questioning, curious and challenging.

They were each members of a leadership team in a complex scenario. They led the IT function of the organisation that needed to provide infrastructure, tools and support to meet the stretching demands of today and, at the same time, plan and build towards the rapidly changing and rapidly approaching demands of tomorrow.

There were clearly a lot of personality preferences coming through. The talkative team member was always seeing the bigger picture, looking to build off others' ideas and share their vision of the future. In reality her functional role needed her to do some of this, some of the time, but not all of the time.

The quieter team member found these contributions over-complicated things, frequently causing discussions to broaden when they needed to come to conclusion, and to introduce what they saw as unnecessary and unwelcome diversions.

Once we started to discuss personality, strengths and roles, lightbulbs very quickly came on for both of them. With sufficient tolerance and acceptance they were able to both quickly make adjustments to provide what each other needed and get the best out of each other, without pretty much any of the previous downsides.

Not so much a personality clash as misunderstanding.

Once you get into the world of work, you'll hear about Myers-Briggs types, Disc styles, and many more ways of describing different personalities. Many people are a little sceptical about what you can get out of putting people into anything between 4 and 16 fairly crude boxes – after all, we're all unique individuals and incredibly different. Life experiences, genetics, skills all shape us into unique personalities.

That said, I've worked with individuals before where there has been a complete clash of styles and approaches. Understanding that they had incredibly different styles and strengths when they did a leadership styles analysis allowed them to have a better understanding for how each other needed to receive and digest information and make decisions. Knowing how each other worked best didn't remove all of the friction, but it certainly made life easier.

> Have you ever used working style analysis to understand your colleagues?
>
> How did it help you work together?

Coping when your workload doubles

A divisional Finance Director I was once coaching had all the normal challenges – pressures, challenges, not enough time, stretched, working longish hours etc, etc...

Then part way through our work together he got asked to take on the role of Group IT Director, as well as his finance role. I think I was more surprised and incredulous than he was, and to start with I couldn't get my head around how he could possibly do both. Needless to say it was the topic of our next 1-1 coaching session where I was able to help him put some sort of plan together to cope, but also to do a great job.

The first thing we did was set some reasonable expectations of what might be possible for him. We then talked about the importance of communication by him to both his teams – the existing one and new one – and his peers in his leadership team. And we talked about the importance of clarity in his role – not just in his head, but in everyone else's too – so that there was a shared picture of the challenges on him and his time, and how he planned to keep his head above water (and swim forward).

Quite quickly we realised the importance of his existing team understanding and accepting how little he was going to be around, compared to before, and the implications for them in their own roles i.e. the need for them to 'step up', attend different meetings, to make bigger decisions - without referral - than they had done before and, just like he had done, to take on more responsibility.

Clarity of roles was the decisive factor in what proved to be a successful period for him and his teams.

I read an account once a of a senior leader starting a new role in an organisation. They sent a memo round explaining how they worked best, and the best ways to engage with them. Apparently it worked very well. Just like in Jim's story, explaining what they needed from the teams around them in a clear and upfront way meant that everyone was on the same page and could do what was needed.

I've also recently read the government commissioned report into a (previous) Lord Chancellor and Foreign Secretary, Dominic Raab. He was accused of behaving in an inappropriate and abusive manner towards staff. One of the accusations was that in the emergency situation surrounding the evacuation of British forces from Afghanistan, he refused to review and approve documents listing priority candidates for evacuation because they weren't in his preferred document layout format.

It just goes to show that whilst being clear and upfront about what you need as a leader is important, that for most people it would go without saying that there are times when things can't be exactly as you'd like. Many people in Raab's situation would get on with the job in hand, accepting that circumstances meant that urgency was more important than formatting.

> How do you ensure that those around you know best how you like to work, and how do you approach things that are not done in an ideal way for good reasons?

Everyone in a team contributing and taking responsibility

One of the best leaders I've ever worked with in my role as a performance coach was a master at calm, collective decision making to help the team he led make the most of their collective potential.

Their job titles, or roles, were just a starting point, because they were such a cohesive unit, and they had developed such high levels of trust and openness, that they were able to freely discuss who was best doing what.

I clearly remember one meeting where the business was starting a new project and the project needed one of his team to spend, potentially, quite a considerable amount of their time supporting it.

The conversation that followed was a masterpiece in shared responsibility, looking to account for individual and collective needs. As different people offered why they might be the best to support the project – reluctantly in some cases, because it offered limited development opportunity or because it meant giving up something else they were already really invested in – other people agreed or disagreed, each time looking to support or challenge the option in a totally constructive way.

People were considering, at the same time, the interests of the project, the interests of the business function that the leadership team led and the interests of the individuals.

It was a pleasure to watch and made me reflect on the ingredients that had enabled them to get to the point where they could operate that way. Putting the team first was one, minimal egos was another, and calm, rational decision making was a third.

Being part of a team that is cohesive, fully trusts each other, and is working 'in flow' is absolutely brilliant. Whether it is people stepping up to take on each push forwards, or agreeing to leave things behind because it isn't the right time, it's a great feeling to know you can rely on those around you to help the collective achieve a goal.

When I played rugby, it was pretty straightforward to understand why the team might be working well together; everyone would know their job and their place, everyone was willing to go above and beyond that role where needed to help the team, and they could do it in a way that didn't stop someone else doing their role.

Sometimes it's harder to see things as clearly as Jim's rundown in a work situation – putting the team first, minimal egos, calm decision making. But when it doesn't work out – someone going their own way, people putting their ego before the team and trying to claim credit or take charge, or arguments about decisions, it can get tricky.

I've worked with people where something has faltered – whether it has been them going and doing something different to what was agreed, or acting without consulting the team. It's amazing how quickly trust can fall apart if they are defensive or not upfront about what they've done. And at the same time, in a trusting team environment it can be fairly straightforward to get back on track by coming back to putting the team first, egos aside, and focusing on the collective end goal rather than blame.

When have you been in a great team with everyone contributing?

How did it feel?

What part did you play?

What do you think really made it a great team?

When have you seen a potentially good team effort turn sour?

What happened and why did things work out that way?

When to refer to your boss or others in making decisions

Of all the businesses I've worked, coached and consulted in, three stand out as the most highly pressured.

One was a UK delivery firm where constant short term deadlines, service standards and competitor pricing caused the strain. One was a UK construction company where financial and time pressures, scale and complexity were the key stressors. And one was a high quality manufacturing business where the main driver, by my reckoning, was the ambition and high standards set by nearly all the employees – irrespective of roles and functions. Everyone was proverbially pushing the boundaries and this caused great tensions.

A regular requirement in that manufacturing business was the ability to make quick decisions without the luxury of necessarily consulting peers or more senior managers.

One group of managers came up with their own process for deciding whose decision and when:

1. Decisions that I can get on and make on my own and are small enough that I don't need to tell my boss or peers – we can just crack on
2. . Decisions that I can get on and make but once made I need to tell my boss and peers what I have decided
3. Decisions that are mine to make but I need to get the input of my boss or peers first
4. Decisions that are not mine to make, but I need my boss or peers to make (and I can be proactive in inputting to them or telling them when I need a decision by)

Often new leader managers, or more experienced leader managers in new roles or surroundings, aren't quite sure where these boundaries lie.

The above four steps can really help with those grey areas, especially when there is an early two way discussion about how and when the four steps can be applied.

I recently chaired a meeting for a colleague who had set the agenda and included several items they wanted to raise. When I got to the part of the agenda with their items, they couldn't decide whether to speak then or wait until later in the meeting, and wanted me to decide for them. Without knowing the detail of what they were planning to discuss and why they might want to delay, I couldn't make that decision. Their knowledge of the situation was far better than mine, and my facilitation role did not change my insight into their situation. My colleague thought it was a Decision Level 4, on Jim's scale above. I knew that it was a Decision Level 1 or maybe 2.

In a past role, someone I line managed turned up to work one day feeling a little under the weather with a cold. They arrived into the office, told me they were feeling unwell, and asked me to decide whether they should stay and work or go home. I told them it was up to them, as they were the only person who knew how bad they felt and whether they were well enough to be at work. Again, they felt it was a Level 4 decision, but it was a level 2 – they just needed to let me know if they had to go home.

My colleagues in these examples wanted help in making decisions they could have made themselves, but part of their indecision was inexperience; they needed someone with greater experience to explain why they had the power to make a decision.

> How do you help others when they are struggling to make the right choice on decision boundaries?
>
> And how do you know where the boundaries lie?

What is your role? How clear are you?

My elder brother worked for many years for a brewery. He started there as one of their earliest employees, doing the books etc as a part qualified accountant. As they and he grew he went on to become Company Secretary and Finance Director.

Some Christmases we would meet as a large family at my parents' house. Steve used to get bottled beer at a staff discount so one year I texted him:

Hi Steve, any chance you could bring some beer for me?

Sure.

I think they come in cases of 12 bottles?

That's right.

Cool I'll have one of those please.

Would you like two cases?

Yes go on then.

I should be in Sales.

Steve, if you work for the company, you are in Sales.

It's a good example of getting so focused in your role - and narrow - that you can lose sight of the bigger picture. And that's rich coming from me. I'm a fine one to talk as I know I can often get narrow in my thinking.

If you work for a company you immediately have a broad role as well as a more specific one.

Back in my rugby days, I'd often get into a difference of opinion with some of the other players. I knew my role, as a member of the front row, was to take part in scrums and lineouts, and help to form rucks and mauls to protect our ball in open play. Sometimes, being a bit slow around the pitch, a ruck or maul would form with most of the other forwards already in. I would stay out of it, standing just behind the fly-half ready for when the ball came out so I could support the backs in the next play and help form the next ruck or maul.

Sometimes the 10 or 12 would yell at me to go and join the existing breakdown. I'd point out that then they'd have no support for the next play. They'd often point out that if the ball didn't come out on our side because I hadn't helped out, there wouldn't be a next play to support!

We never quite fully agreed — I was still not convinced that adding an eighth person to a breakdown with seven of my own team already in it would make that much difference — but we all had a clear understanding of my role on the team. I'd say that I had a better perspective of the bigger picture — but undoubtedly my friends in the back line would say the same thing!

It's not always easy to see the big picture; too few people seeing the big picture risks everyone getting hung up on the exact boundaries of their role and finding there are gaps between them. Too much focus on the big picture can mean we neglect the details and end up without a big picture at all.

How do you find the balance between focusing on your role and seeing it as part of the wider picture and the whole game?

How do you take on board other perspectives about your role?

Developing a way to challenge your challenging boss

As a young consultant I once worked for a period with a particular Regional Manager and his team of Sales Managers. At that time the division was led by a newish and particularly alpha male Sales Director.

In one meeting with the Regional Director and his team we took an impromptu diversion – which would have been led by them not me! – to discuss how they could effectively challenge some of the thinking and decisions of the Sales Director. They were reluctant to do so because of how he was likely to respond.

We came up with a process which, because it was generated by the team, they were pleased with and bought into.

We started by listing his anticipated responses to their challenges. Things like:

- Who are you (to challenge me)?
- Who – or what - says so? (What is the evidence you have?)
- So what? (Do I need to be bothered? Should I care?)
- Ok so what do you want me to do about it?

And then we used these for them to build their case and their approach. Something very broadly along the lines of:

"As one of your Sales team in the South Region, we've noticed this trend happening on several occasions, and have investigated further, and we think in time this will happen if we don't keep on top of it so our recommendation is we change course quickly and do xyz..."

The session – which probably took about half an hour - certainly improved their confidence and sense of empowerment. Though there was still nervousness in using this tactic – fingers had been burnt!

And the biggest step was taken by the member of the team who first raised the issue and asked if we could focus on it.

I once found myself in a tricky situation where I realised that my only option was to challenge my boss about something and ask for changes to be made. I felt it was pretty high-stakes and I wasn't quite sure how to approach it. I was luckily able to access some coaching, and the coach and I practised talking through what I needed to say, the phrasing that would allow what I was saying to be non-confrontational, and how to ensure that I was clear in my speech rather than rushing due to stress.

It was really valuable to have that under my belt when I did have the conversation with my boss. I was able to recall my key points and how to phrase them under pressure, and I was comfortable in taking my time to make those points. The outcome wasn't entirely perfect, but my boss did agree to make some of the changes I had asked for.

When have you practiced a difficult conversation with others, and worked out the best way to tackle the situation? How did it help?

How did you feel about the conversation after practising?

Don't help people if it's not helping them

When I was 18 I spent three months volunteering in a Leonard Cheshire home. Leonard Cheshire was one of two official British observers of the nuclear bombing of Nagasaki from the support B-29 he was flying in.

After the war he founded a charity to support people with a

disability. The home I worked in had about 30-40 residents with severe disabilities, many bedbound or in wheelchairs and most not able to do too much for themselves. One or two had electric wheelchairs but they were very much in the minority.

One of the residents, Barry or Henry – his face is more familiar than his name, with his national health specs and his arms twisted over his lap, fingers contorted – was a pipe smoker. If you walked past him anytime during the day he would invariably call you over to refill his pipe. This meant cleaning it out, getting the tobacco out of the pouch in his pocket, putting the pipe in his mouth and lighting it.

Now I had never smoked, and never used a lighter. I didn't know that once you had spun the metal wheel you only had to hold down the black button for the flame to stay lit. If you did what I did, and kept your thumb jammed to wheel, the hot wheel would soon start to burn your finger!

And the trouble was that Barry used to take ages to puff and get the pipe going. I'm sure my pain must have been obvious but he never told me and I never asked!

The point of the story is about another lady who worked there. One of the full time nurses was short, just a little bit older than me, and quite direct in her manner. She told me in no uncertain terms not to pander to any of the residents. She told me not to go filling up Barry's pipe every time he asked or every time I walked past him. She explained that once my three month voluntary stint was finished, if there were no more volunteers for a period, then Barry and others risked losing the ability to do certain tasks. And that would mean she and the other nurse staff would be asked to do more etc.

It was an example of 'use it or lose it', but also a bigger example of dependence, and trying to help someone in the short term but risking the opposite in the longer term.

Another rugby story; at one point we had a new but rather slightly built player join the team. She had no rugby experience and had never played a contact sport, although was apparently a decent cricketer. During her first couple of training sessions everyone went very easy on her as the main concern with a player new to the sport was that they would be frightened off and never come back!

After the first few sessions I stopped going so easy on her and treated her the same as I would treat my teammates – offering resistance when doing tackling drills (with foam tackle pads, so well cushioned!). None of the other senior players were offering any resistance and would chastise me for being too tough, to which I would reply that in a real match no-one would hold back. Unfortunately, this didn't seem to be important and it meant I was the only person offering any sort of resistance in training; the new player even seemed to think I was picking on them.

Suffice to say, in this new player's first match they received the ball, started running, and got carried several metres backwards by a tackler because they weren't expecting to be hit with force. Everyone had known this was a likely outcome but the verbal warnings they'd offered hadn't had the same impact as training properly would have done. Luckily the new player wasn't hurt and carried on playing.

Just as in Jim's situation, my teammates had favoured short-term comfort over long-term pragmatism, and it had not worked out well for the new player.

> When have you made a decision that was easy in the here and now but had longer-term implications? What did you learn from doing so?
>
> What would you change if you faced it again?

Stepping forward to lead

Some of us take the lead readily and naturally, some of us will take the lead when we feel the situation or challenge requires us to.

I once did jury service and was in the jury for two cases. At the end of the first the judge gave us some direction before sending us out to consider our verdict. I felt that the guidance was minimal but it did include something about us finding it helpful to have someone leading the conversation.

Amongst the jury was someone I felt to be very alpha male. As soon as we sat down he was, as anticipated the first to speak. He said "right, let's go round and see what everyone thinks". He then proceeded, starting with the person immediately to his left, to point at us one by one saying "guilty or not guilty?". By the time he got to me, the last, sitting immediately to his right, everyone had said not guilty. I said not guilty too, at which point he said "me too" and pressed the buzzer to invite the clerk of court back in because we had come to a decision.

Suddenly everyone was saying "whoa, we want a chance to at least discuss it!"

When it came to the second case, based on that experience first time round, when we retired to consider the evidence, I was the first to speak, saying I was happy to play the lead role but was equally happy if someone else wanted to do it. They went with me.

The example is to show that whilst stepping forward and leading might not be a default setting for all of us, many of us can show leadership when it is required of us or when we want to.

There's an old military joke about a new recruit joining his platoon and the Sergeant one day lining everyone up and saying he needs a volunteer.

"Anyone wishing to volunteer should take two paces forwards", says the Sergeant. The new recruit isn't sure about stepping forward, so remains standing still but notices that no-one else has stepped forwards either. In fact, he starts to realise that he is standing alone in front of the Sergeant. When the order to take two paces forward to volunteer had come, everyone else had taken two paces backwards. Sometimes you don't even have to step forwards to end up leading!

I was once asked to lead the pack for my rugby team – essentially acting as captain for the forwards and taking decisions about line-out and scrum tactics. I was very honoured to be asked, but I was only asked once. Somehow my rugby brain didn't connect well with my speaking brain in match situations, and whilst I could play rugby absolutely fine and even take the necessary decisions, I couldn't communicate them clearly without a significant pause to get my brain connecting with my voicebox! Happily for everyone involved there were plenty of other people who had the necessary abilities to take on the role.

Sometimes leadership opportunities can come upon us when we don't expect it or when we're not well-suited to them. There's a fine art in both recognising when you can step up and lead because it's needed, but also when you want to lead though you recognise that someone else's skillset is required.

How have you found yourself stepping forward to lead?

What did you learn from doing so?

Have you ever had to step back from a leadership position and let someone else take things forward?

How did that feel?

What helped you make that decision?

---

14 STRENGTHS

"Persistence is the twin sister of excellence. One is a matter of quality, the other a matter of time."

"So many of us choose our path out of fear disguised as practicality. What we really want seems impossibly out of reach and ridiculous to expect, so we never dare to ask the universe for it. I'm saying that I am the proof that you can ask the universe for it... I learned many great lessons from my father–not the least of which is that you can fail at what you don't want, so you might as well take a chance on doing what you love."

JIM CARREY

Playing to strengths rather than working on weaknesses – or at least before working on weaknesses – seems like an instinctively sensible strategy. I would rather know the strengths of my team mates than their weaknesses. And I would rather be thinking – it would be more helpful to me – about what I am good at than what I am not.

Find ways to contribute based on what you are good at

On a performance programme I was once observing we were joined as a guest by an ex- Olympic rower. I remember at some point the conversation was on the subject of self-talk and she laughed, before sharing with the group that in her first race in a GB vest she rowed to the start line repeating the words "don't screw up, don't screw up". Helpful, she said, but not the most helpful self-talk ever.

The other story she shared was about finding her place in the team.

She knew she was keen to add something from the start, even as the junior rower in the boat, and managed to find a way to do her bit. She was very organised, and also knew the importance of refuelling after racing and training. She was always good at having her drinks bottle to hand and managed to quickly develop into a role in supporting others to do the same.

It was a small example but a good one, to show how even a relative novice can add some value to an older, more experienced team.

It isn't always easy to find your place in the team and show how you can add value. Every season when I played rugby, some people would leave and others would join. One season a new player came along for summer training fresh out of university, and started our first game of the year. She made an excellent impression but very unfortunately broke her leg in that first match, putting her on crutches for months and ruling her out of any more games. As a new player, reliant on public transport and finding it tricky to get around London, she could have easily focused on her recovery and stayed at home on Sundays.

Instead, she came to every game including away fixtures, attended socials, and often brought some baking for the team to enjoy after matches. She became a valuable and much-loved part of the team despite not being able to play any rugby.

Just as Jim's story shows you don't have to be experienced to add value, this story highlights how you don't even have to be 'on the pitch' to help the team move forwards.

How have you found ways to fit in and add value in new environments? Was there an obvious need, or did you have to make your own role?

How did it feel to know your efforts were important to the team?

Quiet - The Power of Introverts in a World that Can't Stop Talking

Susan Cain's story, as told in her book Quiet, and her TED talk 'The Power of Introverts', will have struck a chord with many people.

Her story is about being naturally introverted in a western world that appears to more highly value and appreciate extrovert tendencies – like expressing your emotions, verbalising your thoughts, arguing your case in a debate and social interaction.

Her book Quiet is subtitled 'The Power of Introverts in a World that Can't Stop Talking'. For people who are naturally introverted it can be a reassuring read – that they are ok. It can make them realise that to not be confident to talk in front of the class is perfectly normal, or that to prefer hobbies on your own is quite acceptable.

One of my children is particularly quiet and private. Teachers at parents' evening would say things like "he is clever and intelligent but he could do with speaking up more in class and sharing his ideas". Sometimes I would say "why is that?" and I would repeat the question when they answered. I never got a totally satisfactory answer.

Clearly I can see that there are some situations where it helps to put in the effort to be, say, more talkative. But I think being you, and playing to your strengths, is a more powerful notion.

Jim's story of parents evening reminds me of an anecdote relayed to me after my Mum got home from a school parents evening where she had met my German teacher, Frau R. I really enjoyed learning German and it seemed to come easily to me, and I got on well with Frau R. I was in the top set of the year and routinely got As for my work, and I definitely wasn't shy about putting my hand up with the answers in class.

My German teacher, Frau R, had apparently told my Mum that I was very good and would do well in my GCSE's. However, because I didn't have a conversation partner in lessons they might have to move me down a set. This rather surprised my Mum, given what had been said about my performance. As a languages teacher herself, she asked Frau R how many students were in the class. Frau R admitted that there were an odd number of students in the class and it therefore wasn't actually possible for me to pair up with anyone. Moving me down a set was not discussed again, and the following year the sets had even numbers so that no-one else found themselves in that situation.

This might seem a bit of a tangent from Jim's point that there is value in being yourself, whether that is quiet or more talkative. However intelligent Jim's son was, the teachers wanted him to show his strengths in a manner suited to the classroom environment even when that didn't work well for him. In my case, there was a risk I would be essentially punished for a classroom environment that could never work perfectly for me, because it was impossible.

Jim's point was that playing to your strengths can be much more valuable than being wholly dictated by the environment or situation. Mine is that it's always worth thinking about the environment and situation, and whether it is suited to your strengths.

If it's not working for you, is it able to, and can you change anything?

What is the best way to use your strengths?

Using strengths to tackle weaknesses

"If you want something doing give it to a busy person" is the old adage. I coached someone once who completely fitted the bill.

She was energetic, enthusiastic, busy, warm, efficient and helpful. Her helpfulness, to please people, combined with her energy and her great capability meant she got asked to do more and more. Her bosses valued her and she found it difficult to say no.

One time when we met she was particularly frazzled. She was a keen swimmer – to get exercise, and recover from the strains and stresses of her day – but she had been too busy to do this recently. Her manager had asked her to take on more responsibility, and she was stretched.

Amongst her many strengths was her organisation and planning, and we came up with the simple strategy of using strengths to tackle weaknesses. In this case using her planning and organisation to mitigate against always saying yes.

Stopping to plan, to see what she had on her plate, and to estimate what needed to be done, when, and how much time it would take, enabled her to be proactive in planning her way out of trouble. It even meant she was in a position to go back to her boss and talk to him about priorities.

Using strengths to deal with weaknesses is a strategy I've used with others since.

Way back when I was at school, I had to choose a technology GCSE course. Not being overly practical or artistic, I'd requested to do a systems electronics course, but the school didn't have enough interest from students to run it. I found myself spending two years studying Graphic Design, something I didn't feel particularly comfortable with! Luckily, the growth of desktop publishing software came unexpectedly to my rescue.

I remember being tasked to design a greetings card as homework during the first year of the course. Not being able to draw at all well, I turned to the computer to design something and added a joke to the cover with the punchline inside. I reckoned it looked OK, and handed it in.

At the start of the next lesson, the teacher reviewed some notable examples of good work in the homework task. I was surprised to see her pick my card up and show it to the class. She pointed out that I had not let my lack of artistic talent prevent me from completing the task, but by being able to use the available software and my sense of humour, I'd found ways to meet the brief successfully without actually having to draw anything.

When it comes to having trouble saying no, a former colleague of mine shared some great advice with me. At the point of having to say no, have a 'rule' that prevents you from doing the thing you are saying no to. Whether it's a 'rule' that you don't have a drink after 8pm on a worknight or that you don't take on extra tasks until the project deadline has passed, people find it much easier to accept you are 'bound' by a rule that is causing you to say no.

When have you used your strengths to mitigate your weaknesses?

How have you found successful ways to say no?

CONCLUSION

You've just read – or flicked through - over a hundred stories about different experiences that we've had over the years, at work and in life. Some of those experiences might - we hope - have resonated with you or reminded you of particular moments. Others might have been interesting but felt less personal or relevant.

As we've written down these stories, we've both reflected not just on those experiences we mentioned, and what they meant to us at the time, but also what we have learned from having them as part of our careers and our lives.

The stories in this book are a mix of the very personal and those already very much in the public domain - like Covey's paradigm shift example. Irrespective of their source they all have the power to move us, either emotionally, mentally or very practically.

Stories prompt and provoke thoughts and feelings. They come up in a coaching context because someone has said something that prompts a story. In the telling it can help the listener to later remember the feeling of the learning or provoke further thought.

So many stories are told and retold because there is an element of learning – of human error or adventure that has eventually led to some kind of moving forward.

We hope that these stories might be useful to you now or in the future, whether you have already faced a situation that we have discussed or happen to some time from now.

In either case we hope that you know that others have found those moments worthy of discussion and reflection, because they're not always straightforward and insight is rarely immediate.

Whilst these stories are small parts of who we are and the roads we've metaphorically walked, they are still important to us. We aren't famous or celebrities, and our stories may not be so different from yours or even those of the person next to you - on the train or in the office. But they are stories worth telling. They are important to share so that we can learn from telling them, and you can find yourself in them. Stories and their telling are, after all, one thing that make us human.

We hope that the stories we have written and tell trigger further thoughts for you that will somehow help or be catalysts or perhaps just lodge somewhere in your mind for future reference. And maybe you will retell one or two to those you know who are interested in taking the time to listen. And maybe you will start or continue to tell your own stories when you think they will be helpful for others to hear.

Whether you read this book and never pick it up again, or whether you keep it somewhere where you can refer to it, we would love you to find meaning somewhere inside it.

www.ingramcontent.com/pod-product-compliance
Lightning Source LLC
Chambersburg PA
CBHW030423290526
45786CB00001B/111